MW00908450

SELF-ESTEEM AND GETTING AHEAD

Barbara J. Braham

Consultant/Professional Public Speaker
Columbus, Ohio

Merle Wood

Education Consultant
Formerly of Oakland Public Schools
Lafayette, California

South-Western Publishing Co.

Acquisitions Editor: Karen Schneiter
Series Editor: Mark Linton
Production Editor: Daniel Van
Designer: Darren Wright
Marketing Manager: Shelley Battenfield
Editorial production by: Cinda Johnston

South-Western Publishing Co. gratefully acknowledges the foresight and commitment that Ben Willard, Acquisitions Editor, gave to this LIFE Series.

Copyright © 1992
by SOUTH-WESTERN PUBLISHING CO.
Cincinnati, Ohio

ALL RIGHTS RESERVED

The text of this publication, or any part thereof, may not be reproduced or transmitted in any form or by any means, electronic or mechanical, including photocopying, recording, storage in an information retrieval system, or otherwise, without the prior written permission of the publisher.

1 2 3 4 5 6 7 8 H 8 7 6 5 4 3 2 1

Braham, Barbara J.
   Self-esteem and getting ahead / Barbara J. Braham, Merle Wood.
      p. cm. -- (Life series)
   Includes index.
   ISBN 0-538-70572-8
   1. Self-respect.   2. Self-realization.   3. Self-respect--Problems,
exercises, etc.   4. Self-realization--Problems, exercises, etc.
I. Wood, Merle W.   II. Title.   III. Series: Life series (Cincinnati,
Ohio)
BF697 .5.S46B73   1992
158' .1--dc20

91-34034
CIP

 This book is printed on acid-free paper that meets the Environmental Protection Agency standards for recycled paper.

PREFACE

Basic skills are required for each of us to conduct our personal and business dealings. An increasing need exists to provide adults with these basic skills so they can improve both their personal interactions and employment opportunities.

As a result, the LIFE Series was developed because South-Western believes that **Learning Is For Everyone** (**LIFE**). The LIFE Series is specifically designed to provide adults with the basic skills needed for personal dealings and for job opportunities.

THE LIFE SERIES

The LIFE Series is a self-paced, competency-based program specifically designed for adults to develop basic skills for job and personal use. Each book in the Series provides interesting material, realistic examples, practical applications, and flexible instruction to promote learner success and self-confidence.

The LIFE Series is divided into three basic skill areas—communication skills, math skills, and life skills. SELF-ESTEEM AND GETTING AHEAD is one of the life skills books in the LIFE Series. Each text-workbook is complete and may be used individually or in a series. The following is a complete list of the LIFE Series.

Communication Skills

Spelling for Job and Personal Use
Reading for Job and Personal Use
Grammar and Writing for Job and Personal Use
Punctuation, Capitalization, and Handwriting
        for Job and Personal Use
Listening and Speaking for Job and Personal Use

Math Skills

Basic Math for Job and Personal Use
Decimals, Fractions, and Percentages
        for Job and Personal Use
Calculator Math for Job and Personal Use

Life Skills

Career Planning and Development
Problem Solving and Decision Making for Job and Personal Use
Self-Esteem and Getting Ahead
Money Management
Finding and Holding a Job

STRUCTURE AND ORGANIZATION

Each book in the LIFE Series has the same appearance and structure, enabling learners to experience more success and gain self-confidence as they progress. Competency-based instruction is also used throughout by first presenting clear objectives followed by short segments of material with specific exercises for immediate reinforcement.

The organization of SELF-ESTEEM AND GETTING AHEAD reflects the step-by-step process a person goes through to raise his or her self-esteem. In Part One, Understanding Self-Esteem, students learn the difference between self-esteem and self-image, where self-esteem comes from, and why it fluctuates. Part Two, The Causes of Low Self-Esteem, describes how self-esteem is eroded through judgment, comparison, perfectionism, negative thinking, and irrational beliefs. Students learn how to stop these behaviors that are the cause of many of their feelings of low self-esteem. In Part Three, Build Your Self-Esteem, students learn how to raise their level of self-esteem by knowing and accepting themselves, and by learning to use positive self-talk.

The Glossary, Index, Answers, and Personal Progress Record at the end of SELF-ESTEEM AND GETTING AHEAD are designed to facilitate and enhance independent student learning and achievement.

SPECIAL FEATURES OF SELF-ESTEEM AND GETTING AHEAD

SELF-ESTEEM AND GETTING AHEAD is a complete and comprehensive package providing the student with learning material written specifically to meet the unique needs of the adult learner and providing the instructor with support materials to facilitate student success. Some special features include the following:

Design Characteristics. Each text-workbook in the LIFE Series, including SELF-ESTEEM AND GETTING AHEAD, uses perforated pages and a larger typeface to make it easier for the student to use and to read.

Appropriate Content. Real-life issues and skills are emphasized throughout the text, with relevant examples and illustrations provided to which the student can relate.

Objectives. Instructional objectives are clearly stated for each unit, letting students know what they will learn.

Checkpoints. Checkpoints follow short segments of instruction and provide students with an opportunity to immediately use what they have just learned.

Goals. Goals are listed for each exercise to give the student motivation and direction.

Study Breaks. Each unit contains study breaks that provide a refreshing break from study and yet contribute to the global literacy goal of the student.

Summaries. A summary of the student's accomplishments is provided at the end of each unit, providing encouragement and reinforcement.

Putting It Together. The end-of-unit activities cover the theories presented in the Checkpoints and provide goals for students to measure their own skill development and success.

Glossary. Important terms in the text are printed in bold and defined the first time they are used. These terms are listed and defined in the Glossary for easy reference.

Answers. Answers for all the Checkpoints and Activities are provided at the back of the text-workbook and designed for easy reference to facilitate independent and self-paced learning.

Personal Progress Record. Students keep track of their own progress by recording scores on a Personal Progress Record. Students can measure their own success by comparing their scores to evaluation guides provided for each unit. Whenever a student's total score for a unit is below the minimum requirement, the student may request a Bonus Exercise from the instructor.

SPECIAL FEATURES OF THE INSTRUCTOR'S MANUAL

The Instructor's Manual provides general instructional strategies and specific teaching suggestions for SELF-ESTEEM AND GETTING AHEAD along with supplementary bonus exercises and answers, testing materials, and a certificate of completion.

Bonus Exercises. Second-chance exercises for all activities are offered through bonus exercises provided in the Instructor's Manual. These bonus exercises enable instructors to provide additional applications to those students whose scores are less than desirable for a unit. Answers to all bonus exercises are also provided and can be duplicated for student use.

Testing Materials. Four assessment tools, entitled Checking What You Know, are provided. These tests may be used interchangeably as pretests or post-tests allowing for flexible use.

Certificate of Completion. Upon completion of SELF-ESTEEM AND GETTING AHEAD, a student's success is recognized through a certificate of completion. This certificate has a listing of topics that were covered in the program. A master certificate is included in the manual.

SELF-ESTEEM AND GETTING AHEAD is designed specifically to help you invest in your adult learners' futures and to meet your instructional needs.

ACKNOWLEDGEMENTS

Special thanks to Rick Sullivan and Ben Willard for their support and encouragement.

CONTENTS

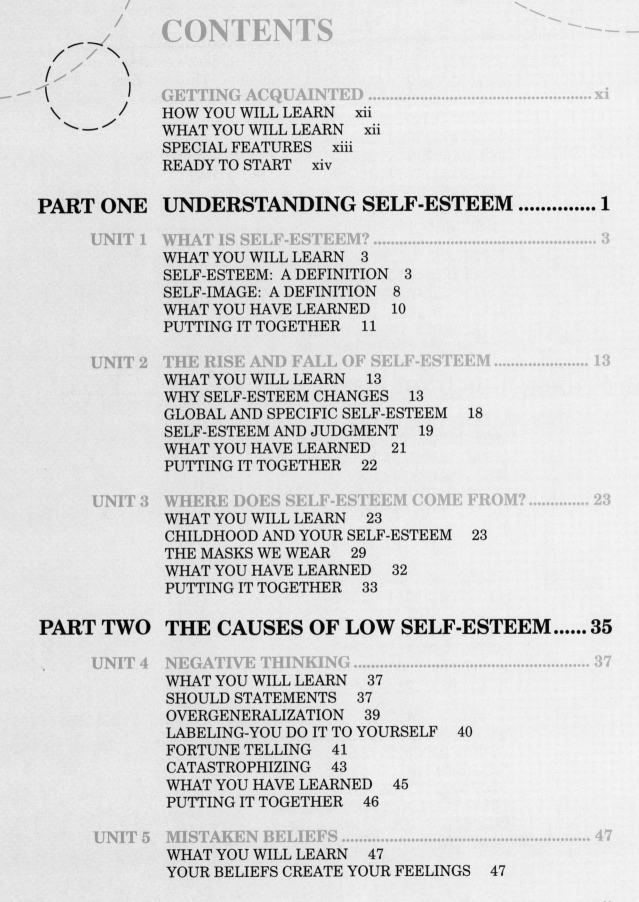

GETTING ACQUAINTED

You want to be happy. You want to feel successful. You want to enjoy your life. These things are all possible when you like yourself—when you have high self-esteem. That's what SELF-ESTEEM AND GETTING AHEAD is about. How to like yourself so that you can create the kind of life you want.

It is so easy to be hard on yourself. You see the mistakes you make. You compare yourself to others. You criticize yourself. It's as if a Judge lives inside of you. The Judge isn't ever satisfied with you as you are. After a while, you can start to wonder if you are okay or not.

This book will show you how the Judge can make you feel bad about yourself. You will learn how to stop judging yourself. You will learn to accept yourself.

After you learn to turn off the Judge, you'll need a new way to talk to yourself. Instead of putting yourself down, you will affirm yourself. Instead of regretting past mistakes, you will set goals for the future. Instead of feeling guilty over what you should do, you'll discover your unique talents and your personal values.

You will have the tools to create the kind of You that you want to be. The You that you can be. It is within your power to change your life. It starts within. It starts with You liking You.

This book provides tools to build high self-esteem and keep it high. It's up to you to study the tools and use them. Learn to feel good about yourself and show it!

Illustration GA-1

Feel Good About Yourself!

HOW YOU WILL LEARN

There is a system used in SELF-ESTEEM AND GETTING AHEAD to help you learn. You need to know how this system works.

Learn at Your Own Pace

You will progress through the lessons on your own. You can move at your own best pace. You may move ahead faster, or go slower, than other students. But, don't be concerned about this. You are to work at your best speed.

Learn Skills Successfully

You are given learning objectives and goals. You will know what you are to accomplish. You will study a topic. Then you will drill over what you have learned. When you have shown that you know the topic, you will move on to the next topic. If you have not learned the topic, you will do added study on that section. You will know just how well you are doing as you move through each step in SELF-ESTEEM AND GETTING AHEAD.

Complete Bonus Exercises

You may not reach your assigned goal on every practice exercise. When this happens, you are asked to review the lesson again and then do a Bonus Exercise. The Bonus Exercises cover the same lesson as the practice exercises in the book. They give you a second chance to reach your goal. When you score higher on a Bonus Exercise than you did on the original exercise, you may change your score on your Personal Progress Record.

Check Your Own Success

You will keep track of your own success. After most activities in the book, you will check your own work. The answers are in the back of the book. Then you will record your score on your own Personal Progress Record. Your record is at the back of the book.

WHAT YOU WILL LEARN

As you study SELF-ESTEEM AND GETTING AHEAD, you will learn how to stop judging yourself and others. You will learn to accept yourself. This will affect how you feel about yourself at home, at work, and with friends. To learn how to build your self-esteem, you will study three parts:

Part One   Understanding Self-Esteem
Part Two   The Causes of Low Self-Esteem
Part Three   Build Your Self-Esteem

Understanding Self-Esteem

In Part One you will learn the difference between self-esteem and self-image. You will find out why your self-esteem changes from one situation to the next. And you will learn how your childhood affects how you feel about yourself today.

The Causes of Low Self-Esteem

The major cause of low self-esteem is judgment. You can judge yourself with negative thinking, by comparing yourself to others, or by being a perfectionist. Sometimes you hold on to irrational beliefs that can lower your self-esteem. In Part Two you will learn how to stop judging yourself, so you can like yourself.

Build Your Self-Esteem

Once you stop tearing yourself down, you need to know how to build yourself up. In Part Three, you will learn how to raise your level of self-esteem. You will learn more about yourself—your values, your talents and skills, your feelings. You will learn how to replace negative thinking with a special type of positive thinking called affirmations. Finally, you will be able to set goals to help you continue feeling good about yourself.

SPECIAL FEATURES ━━━━━━━━━━

SELF-ESTEEM AND GETTING AHEAD has a number of special features. These features will help you learn and apply the material successfully.

Lift Your Spirits

Each unit will have several breaks from the text. The breaks are titled Lift Your Spirits. These breaks will give you exercises you can try that will help build your self-esteem. Sometimes the break will be a quote or poem that is uplifting. The breaks will help you apply what you're learning.

Checkpoints

This book has a number of exercises in each unit called Checkpoints. Each Checkpoint will help you check your understanding of a topic before moving on to the next topic.

Putting It Together

At the end of the units, you will find a section called Putting It Together. This section contains Activities. These are similar to the Checkpoints within the units. They will help you to apply and reinforce the skills you learned in the unit.

Bonus Checkpoints and Activities

If you do not reach the assigned goal for any of the Checkpoints or Activities, you are asked to review the unit. Then you are asked to do a Bonus Checkpoint or Bonus Activity. These give you a second chance to succeed. These second-chance activities are not in this book. Your instructor has copies for you. Your instructor also has the answer key to these activities. You will use it to check your own work.

Answers

Answers to all the exercises and activities are provided in the back of SELF-ESTEEM AND GETTING AHEAD. The answer pages are colored, making them easy to find and use. You will use these pages to check your own work. Always do the exercises and activities before you look at the answers. Use the answers as a tool to verify your work—not as a means of completing the activities.

Personal Progress Record

You will check most of your work with the answers. Then you will record your score on your own Personal Progress Record located at the back of the book. After you complete a unit, you will be able to determine your level of success.

Completion Certificate

When you finish your study in this book you may be eligible for a certificate of completion. Your instructor will explain to you the skill level required for this award.

READY TO START

You are now ready to start building your self-esteem! Throughout this book you will be given the steps to take. Through the guided study and completion of the activities in the book, you will learn to like yourself more and more.

Your new skills will prove to be of benefit to you. The will help you at home and at work. You will feel better about yourself and have more self-confidence. You will be able to create the kind of life you want for yourself. Let's begin!

PART ONE
UNDERSTANDING SELF-ESTEEM

UNIT 1
WHAT IS SELF-ESTEEM?

UNIT 2
THE RISE AND FALL OF SELF-ESTEEM

UNIT 3
WHERE DOES SELF-ESTEEM COME FROM?

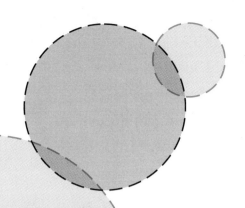

UNIT 1
WHAT IS SELF-ESTEEM?

WHAT YOU WILL LEARN

When you finish this unit, you will be able to:

- Define self-esteem.
- Define self-image.

Do you like yourself? Do you believe you can do anything you set your mind to do? Do you accept other people as they are?

These are all questions about your level of self-esteem. Could you answer "yes" to each question? If not, this book is for you! You can learn to like yourself. You can change your beliefs. You can learn to accept yourself and others.

When you can answer "yes" to each question, you will know you have high self-esteem.

SELF-ESTEEM: A DEFINITION

Self-esteem is how you feel about yourself. When you look at yourself in the mirror in the morning can you say, "I like myself!" Or, do you look in the mirror and think "I'm ugly," or "I wish I was different," or "I don't like myself."

If you don't like yourself very much, you have low self-esteem. If you like yourself most of the time, you have high self-esteem. Most people have self-esteem that is somewhere in the middle. Self-esteem goes up and down like a yo-yo. Some days you wake up, feel great, and the whole day goes great. Other days you start the day feeling bad, and you feel that way all day.

Check Your Self-Esteem

Read through each of the following statements. Put a *T* in the space provided if a statement is true for you. Leave the space blank if it is not true.

1. _____ I can admit a mistake.

2. _____ I can talk to people I don't know.

3. ____ I do what I believe is right even if others don't approve.

4. ____ I can accept a compliment and not feel uncomfortable.

5. ____ I can be myself around other people.

6. ____ I accept myself with all my faults and weaknesses.

7. ____ I can tell you my strengths.

8. ____ I can feel happy for someone else when he or she succeeds.

9. ____ I do not compare myself with others.

10. ____ I have peace of mind.

11. ____ I believe I am unique.

12. ____ I accept differences in others without judging them.

13. ____ I compliment others.

14. ____ I can say "I love you" to all the people I love.

15. ____ I love myself.

16. ____ I am comfortable being alone.

Count the number of statements you marked *True*. If you have 11 or more trues, you have high self-esteem. Answering true to 6-10 statements puts you in middle self-esteem. You have low self-esteem if you had 5 or fewer trues.

However you scored on the checklist you can learn to feel better about yourself. You can have more good days than bad days. You can feel like the people in Illustration 1-1 (page 5) do.

You can usually tell how a person feels about him/herself. You can tell by how you react to the person. If you think to yourself, "Wow! I can't wait to see you again," you were with someone with high self-esteem. Being with him or her makes you feel good about yourself. But, if you think, "Boy, I hope I don't see him/her again soon," you were with someone with low self-esteem. If you didn't feel strongly one way or the other, the person probably had middle self-esteem.

If you have low self-esteem, you are often negative. You don't expect things to work out, and you may even stop trying. You don't feel in control of your life. You react to the things that happen to you with blame and feelings of worthlessness.

Illustration 1-1

Feeling Good Shows

People in the middle need the approval of others. They feel
self-doubt. They hope that the doubt will go away if they can get
others to like them. They listen more to others than to themselves. They are people pleasers.

If you have high self-esteem, you aren't afraid to be yourself.
You can risk being different from the crowd. You can say what
you think and feel. You aren't worried about what other people
will think. Most of the time you feel self-confident. You have a
positive attitude about life and feel in charge of your life.

✔ CHECKPOINT 1-1

YOUR GOAL:
Get 7 or more
answers
correct.

Read the list of words. Decide if they describe a person with high,
middle, or low self-esteem. Write *High*, *Middle*, or *Low* in the
space provided. An example has been completed for you. Give
yourself one point for each correct answer.

●   __High__   risk-taker

1.   _____   trusting

2.   _____   suspicious

3.   _____   unsure

4.   _____   inferior

5.   _____   self-confident

6.   _____   self-doubt

7.   _____   self-hatred

8.   _____   I can

☞ *Check your work. Record your score.*

When you have high self-esteem, you decide that you are a valuable, worthwhile human being. Other people may like and approve of you, or they may not. You don't let them control how you feel about you, though. In other words, your feeling of self-esteem comes from inside of you. You can like you even if someone else doesn't! You can stop trying to please others. You can be yourself!

Self-Worth

Every person has worth. You have worth because you are alive. **Self-worth** is your belief that you are a valuable human being. You feel like you count. If your self-esteem drops, you can feel worthless. When you feel worthless, you think that you don't matter. You feel empty inside.

Some people increase their feelings of self-worth by doing things that they think are worthwhile. They do things that they think will make a difference. For example, if you work outside the home, you might get feelings of self-worth from your job. Tasks that you do at home like fixing the car, cleaning the house, raising children, or growing a garden can also give you self-worth.

Self-Respect

Self-respect is the opinion you have about yourself. If you behave according to what you believe is right, you can respect yourself. But if you believe one thing and act in a different way, you will lose respect for yourself. Loss of self-respect is the first step toward self-hatred.

◀ LIFT YOUR SPIRITS

Think back to a time when you did something that you felt good about. You might have done something for another person. Or you might have achieved something. You could have made something. Remember everything you can about this time when you felt good about yourself. Then complete this sentence: I felt good about myself when _____ because _____.
The next time you feel down on yourself, remind yourself of this time when you felt good.

Values are *your* beliefs about what is right. Different people have different values. Values help you decide what is important in life. For example, you might value honesty. As long as you tell the truth, you will have self-respect. But if you say you value honesty and then you tell lies, you won't respect yourself. If you do the same thing with other values, your self-esteem will suffer because you will lose your self-respect.

Self-Confidence

Self-confidence is believing in yourself. You have an attitude of "I can do it!" You trust yourself. Acting self-confident is difficult if you don't like yourself. If you feel worthless, you won't have self-confidence. One benefit of building your self-esteem is that you will feel more self-confident. When you meet people who are self-confident, you know they believe in themselves.

Self-worth and self-respect are both parts of self-esteem, as you can see in Illustration 1-2. You need self-worth and self-respect to feel good about yourself. When you like yourself, you act self-confident because you feel that way.

Illustration 1-2

Esteem Leads
to Confidence

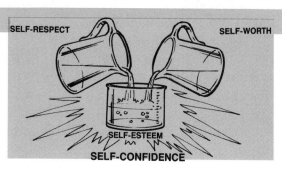

✔ *CHECKPOINT 1-2*

YOUR GOAL:
Get 4 or more answers correct.

Complete the following statements. Write the correct word or words in the space provided. Choose your answer from the list of words provided. An example has been completed for you. Give yourself one point for each correct answer.

self-esteem	self-worth
self-respect	values

● <u>Self-confidence</u> comes when you like yourself.

1. The set of beliefs that you use to tell right from wrong are your _____.

2. If you act different than what you believe is right, you can lose your _____.

3. You may get feelings of _____ from what you do.

4. To have high self-esteem you need both _____ and
    _____.

5. People who appear to be self-confident also have high
    _____.

☞ *Check your work. Record your score.*

SELF-IMAGE: A DEFINITION

Self-image is what you want other people to think of you. Self-image is often confused with self-esteem. The terms are different. Most people are very concerned about what other people think. They want other people to like them. They think that if other people like them, then they will like themselves.

Magazine, radio, and TV ads are designed to make you think that a positive image is the same thing as high self-esteem. Ads give the impression that if you wear a certain brand of clothes or drive a certain car you will be sexy or successful. Have you noticed that if you buy these products, how you *feel* about yourself doesn't change?

Self-image is not the real you. Self-image is an imitation. You try to imitate the people you admire. You try to make people believe you are the person you wish you were. For example, Pedro might be very sensitive and tender as a person. When he watches TV, he sees images of men who are tough and macho. If Pedro tries to be like the TV characters instead of himself, he will become concerned about his "image." He won't be himself.

Concern about his image hurts Pedro in two ways. First, he may not honor his values. To act tough he may do things that conflict with his sensitivity. If he behaves differently from his values, he can lose his self-respect.

Second, even if Pedro is successful creating the macho image, and everyone thinks he is tough, he won't feel good. Why not? Because no one knows the real Pedro. They like the image.

Self-image is a trap. To create a positive self-image is often to destroy your self-esteem. And, self-image makes you an addict. You become addicted to the opinions of other people. You look for them to tell you that you are "okay." You become addicted to what's "in." To be accepted, you change with each new fad. Liking yourself comes from the outside in. *If* others like you, *then* you can like yourself.

With self-image, whether you like yourself or not *depends*. Liking yourself depends on if you have the things the TV or radio says you need to be okay. It depends on what your friends and co-workers think about you. And liking yourself depends on what your family believes about you. You may never measure up. If you have self-esteem, liking yourself comes from the inside out. Others like you because you like yourself.

If you *try* to have a positive self-image, you will try to impress other people. You will try to meet their expectations, hoping to be accepted. If you have high self-esteem, you will accept yourself and others. You will be true to yourself.

Some people try so hard to project a positive image that the opposite happens. They brag, seem selfish, act superior, and talk about themselves most of the time. You may feel like you want to get away from them. When you are around someone with high self-esteem, you feel good about yourself. You want to be around the high self-esteem person again and again.

LIFT YOUR SPIRITS

Napoleon Hill studied people who were successful in the 1920s and 1930s. He wrote a book about what he learned called <u>Think and Grow Rich</u>. Millions of people read his book and learned how to be successful. Napoleon Hill said, "If you think you can, or if you think you can't, you're right."

CHECKPOINT 1-3

YOUR GOAL:
Get 8 or more answers correct.

Read each of the following statements. Decide if a statement describes self-esteem or self-image. Write the word *Esteem* or *Image* in the space provided. An example has been completed for you. Give yourself one point for each correct answer.

-    <u>Esteem</u>   How you feel about yourself.

1. _____ I like myself.

2. _____ I can outdrink anyone.

3. _____ You make choices based on what you believe is right.

4. _____ I believe I can do what I decide I want to do.

5. _____ You try to impress other people.

6. _____ I accept myself.

7. _____ I compare myself to others.

8. _____ You worry about what other people will think.

9.   _____   I have worth as a person.

10.   _____   I try to be who other people want me to be.

☞ *Check your work. Record your score.*

Self-esteem comes from knowing and accepting yourself as you are. You stop trying to be someone you are not. When you don't accept yourself, you wish you were someone else. That is the image you try to project. You compare yourself with the person you wish you were, and you don't measure up. You feel there is something wrong with you. As long as who you are doesn't match with who you wish you were, you will feel emotional pain.

Where does the ideal person that you wish you were come from? From other people's expectations. Those people are usually parents, teachers, and others who were important to you when you were young. They told you how you *should* think, feel, and act. They did not always accept you as you were.

Your ideal self may also come from television or magazines. You may wish you were like a movie star, or a person you see pictured in a magazine.

When you have high self-esteem, you like who you are. You don't try to be someone else. You try to be the best that you can be.

LIFT YOUR SPIRITS

You can start today to change how you feel about yourself. How? By saying "I like myself" at least three times each morning and evening. Saying these words will feel strange at first. After a week or so, they will be easier to say. After a month, you will start to feel different about yourself. Try it!

WHAT YOU HAVE LEARNED

Self-esteem is how you feel about yourself. When you have self-worth and self-respect, your self-esteem is high. People with high self-esteem seem confident. Self-image is different from self-esteem. Your self-image comes from trying to please others. You try to meet others' expectations of you. When you *try* to have a good image, you lower your self-esteem.

ACTIVITY 1-1 **YOUR GOAL:** Get 8 or more answers correct.

Complete each of the following statements. Write the correct word or words in the space provided. Choose your answer from the list of words provided. An example has been completed for you. Give yourself one point for each correct answer.

depends	image	low	middle
self-esteem	self-image	self-worth	values

● People who like themselves have high <u>self-esteem</u>.

1. If you don't take risks, see the negative side of things, and feel worthless, you have _____ self-esteem.

2. If your self-esteem bounces like a yo-yo, you probably have _____ self-esteem.

3. When you try to be someone you aren't, you are concerned about your _____.

4. You can destroy your _____ with your self-image.

5. With _____, you think that if others like you, you will like yourself.

6. When you accept who you are, you have high _____.

7. Achieving or accomplishing something adds to your feelings of _____.

8. Most advertising wants you to project a positive _____.

9. Your image _____ on what other people think.

10. People with high self-esteem act according to their _____, or beliefs, not according to what other people will think.

☞ *Check your work. Record your score.*

ACTIVITY 1-2 **YOUR GOAL:** Get 8 or more answers correct.

Read each of the following statements. Choose the answer that is correct. Write the letter in the space provided. An example has been completed for you. Give yourself one point for each correct answer.

● __c__ Which one of these words is not related to self-esteem?
  a. self-confidence
  b. self-worth
  c. self-image

1. _____   Which word describes someone with high self-esteem?
              a. confident
              b. negative
              c. blaming

2. _____   Which words describe self-image?
              a. Bounces like a yo-yo
              b. Imitation — who you wish you were
              c. Accept yourself

3. _____   Which words describe how a person with a positive image may
              show low self-esteem?
              a. Brags, acts superior, talks a lot
              b. Confident, listens, trusts
              c. Smart, good job, lots of friends

4. _____   A person trapped by an image is addicted to:
              a. drugs
              b. approval
              c. TV

5. _____   What is self-respect?
              a. You act according to your values
              b. You can prove yourself to someone
              c. You achieve something

6. _____   Which of these activities would give you a feeling of self-worth?
              a. Reading a book
              b. Planting a garden
              c. a & b

7. _____   Which phrase does not describe self-image?
              a. The person you wish you were
              b. High self-esteem
              c. The person you think you should be

8. _____   Self-confidence
              a. Is knowing you are a valuable human being
              b. Comes from other people
              c. Is believing in yourself

☞ *Check your work. Record your score.*

UNIT 2
THE RISE AND FALL OF SELF-ESTEEM

WHAT YOU WILL LEARN

When you finish this unit, you will be able to:

- Explain why self-esteem changes in different situations.
- Define global and specific self-esteem.
- Identify the difference between a fact and a judgment.

Your self-esteem often acts like a yo-yo. Sometimes you feel good about yourself. At other times you don't like yourself. Sometimes you feel self-confident. Other times you feel scared and insecure. What causes these changes in how you feel about yourself?

WHY SELF-ESTEEM CHANGES

Your level of self-esteem is affected by three things. First, the skills you have will affect how you feel about yourself. Your skills make you feel capable. Second, inside you there is a Judge who will put you down if you will listen. And last, the people you spend time with can affect your self-esteem.

Self-Esteem And Your Skills

You learned many skills as you grew up. There are many things that you can do. Your skills give you a feeling of "I can!" When you are in a situation where you can use the skills you have, you feel good about yourself. Like the people in Illustration 2-1, you can proudly say, "I did it!"

Illustration 2-1

"I Did It!"

Imagine that you know how to work on cars. Your friend, Ralph, has a problem with his car. You would feel good about yourself knowing that you could help Ralph. Your self-esteem would rise in this situation.

But what if someone asks for help solving a math problem? Maybe you don't understand fractions, and you don't know how to find the answer. Then you might feel badly about yourself. Your self-esteem might drop. Rather than feeling confident, you might feel embarrassed.

Maybe you are very good at your job. You might get compliments from your boss and coworkers about your work. While you are at work, you feel good about yourself. You have high self-esteem. But when you go home, you fight and have trouble getting along with the rest of the family. Because you don't have good communication skills, your self-esteem drops in this situation.

One reason your self-esteem rises and falls, then, has to do with your skills. When you know how to do something, you feel better about yourself than when you don't. Being able to do something adds to your feelings of self-worth. You feel valuable, and that builds your self-esteem.

Self-Esteem And The Judge

During a single day you have many feelings about yourself. You might feel good about getting up on time and getting to work on time. Then you might be put on a new piece of equipment that you don't know how to use. Your self-esteem might drop. When you help a friend solve a problem, you feel good again. At home

◄
◄
◄

LIFT YOUR SPIRITS

Criticizing ourselves is so easy to do! We often think about what's wrong with us instead of what's right. Take a minute now to think of five things that you like about yourself. These can be big things or small things. You might like the color of your hair, your decision to go to school, how you treat your friends, or how you budget money. Anything. Write your five likes in the space provided. I like myself because:

_____

_____

_____

_____

_____

you can't start the lawn mower, and your self-esteem drops. Then the kids thank you for fixing a broken toy, and your self-esteem soars.

How much your self-esteem bounces in these situations will depend upon the Judge. The **Judge** is a little voice inside of you that tells you all the things you are doing wrong. The Judge says things like "You could do better," and "Why did you do that?" The Judge tells you that you aren't good enough.

Everyone has a Judge inside. People with high self-esteem have learned not to listen to the Judge. When the inner criticism starts, people with high self-esteem say, "Here comes the Judge!" People with low self-esteem listen to the Judge all the time. Listening to the Judge will make you feel bad about yourself.

Whenever you hear the words *should*, *ought*, or *must*, the Judge is talking to you. Those three words are judgmental. **Acceptance** is the opposite of judgment. People with high self-esteem accept themselves. The Judge doesn't accept you as you are. The Judge wants you to be different than you are. The louder the Judge, the more your self-esteem will bounce like a yo-yo.

✔

CHECKPOINT 2-1

YOUR GOAL: Get 4 or more answers correct.

Read each of the following statements. If a statement is true, write a *T* in the space provided. If it is false, write an *F* in the space provided. An example has been completed for you. Give yourself one point for each correct answer.

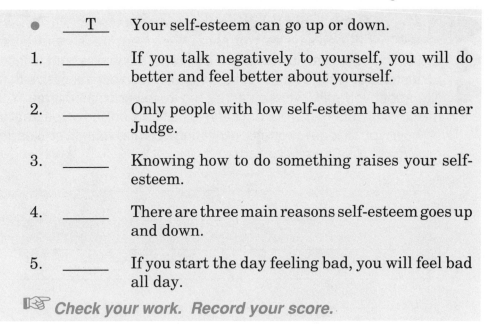

-    __T__   Your self-esteem can go up or down.

1. _____ If you talk negatively to yourself, you will do better and feel better about yourself.

2. _____ Only people with low self-esteem have an inner Judge.

3. _____ Knowing how to do something raises your self-esteem.

4. _____ There are three main reasons self-esteem goes up and down.

5. _____ If you start the day feeling bad, you will feel bad all day.

☞ *Check your work. Record your score.*

Let's look at some examples of how *shoulds* can lower your self-esteem. Imagine that your car overheats. If the Judge starts talking, you might hear something like this:

"You should know how to fix an overheated car! This isn't the first time it's happened. You'd think you would've learned what to do by now. Maybe you shouldn't be driving if you can't handle a simple problem."

Wow! That's a tough Judge. With talk like that you're sure to feel bad for awhile.

At work, when you are asked to use a new piece of equipment the Judge might not say much. Perhaps the Judge won't attack you at all. Your Judge might give you a break and attack your boss instead.

"He should have given me better instructions."

Your self-esteem wouldn't drop. But that night when you burnt the hot dogs on the grill, your Judge might get nasty and say:

"You shouldn't have been watching TV when you were cooking. You should have watched the hot dogs more closely. You shouldn't make such a dumb mistake. What's wrong with you anyway? Now you've wasted food when money was already tight."

LIFT YOUR SPIRITS

Did you know that we need to hear ten positive things for every one negative thing? For most people, the opposite happens. Most people hear ten negatives for every one positive. You can make a difference to other people. Notice when they do something right and tell them about it. You'll feel better about yourself, too.

It is not the situation that affects your self-esteem. What the Judge says to you about the situation is what lowers your self-esteem. In fact, the Judge has more control over how you feel about yourself than anything or anyone else.

You're going to learn how to make the Judge be quiet later in this book. And, you will learn how to create an inner Fan Club. Then you can choose who you listen to — the Judge or your Fan Club. You can take charge of your feelings of self-esteem!

Self-Esteem and Other People

Your self-esteem is affected by the people with whom you spend time. How do you feel about yourself if you are with someone who says things like this to you:

"You never do anything right!"
"You dress so sloppy!"
"What's wrong with you anyway?"
"You'll never get anywhere."

Negatives can cause you not to like yourself. Do you spend time with people who seem to want to destroy your self-esteem instead of build it?

Now imagine how you would feel if you were around someone who said these things to you:

"You can do it!"
"I knew you could figure it out."
"Thank you for your help."
"I enjoy being around you."
"I appreciate all the help you gave me when I was sick."

Don't you think you would feel more positive about yourself? Being around positive people builds your self-esteem.

CHECKPOINT 2-2

YOUR GOAL: Get 5 or more answers correct.

Read each of the following statements. Decide if each statement would raise or lower your self-esteem. In the space provided put a "+" if it would raise your esteem. Put a "-" (minus sign) if it would lower your esteem. An example has been completed for you. Give yourself one point for each correct answer.

● ___—___ You make a mistake, and the Judge says "You should have done it right the first time."

1. _____ Your child asks for help with homework, and you know how to help.

2. _____ A friend says, "You can do it!"

3. _____ A neighbor says, "You're all thumbs, aren't you?"

4. _____   You help a friend with a problem that turns out all right.

5. _____   You go to pay your electric bill, and the person at the counter says, "You should have paid this last week."

6. _____   You repair a tear in the porch screen, and you feel proud of your work.

☞ *Check your work. Record your score.*

We all try to understand who we are based on what we learn about ourselves from other people. Other people become like a mirror. But sometimes those other people don't give us a true picture. They are like a mirror in a fun house, making some parts too big, and other parts too small. That's why *self-esteem is an inside job.* You need to decide for yourself that you are a valuable human being.

Choose the people you spend time with carefully. You don't need people who put you down! You can do that all by yourself when you listen to the Judge.

GLOBAL AND SPECIFIC SELF-ESTEEM

You play many parts or roles in your life. The list in Illustration 2-3 may be just a few of the roles you play.

Illustration 2-3

Roles in Life

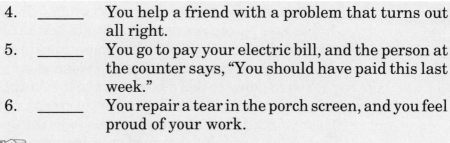

son/daughter	referee	student	decision-maker
parent	entertainer	employee	teacher
cook	counselor	repair person	doctor
breadwinner	listener	lover	cheerleader

You feel good in some of the roles you play. In other roles you don't feel as good. Any role in which you feel good about yourself gives you **specific self-esteem**. In other words, in that specific role you like yourself. You feel self-confident — you can do it!

Global self-esteem is how you feel about yourself overall. In general, do you like yourself or not? You don't think about any specific role. Instead, you look at the big picture. Are you a lovable person? If the answer is yes, you have high global self-esteem.

If you have global self-esteem, you can still have low self-esteem in a specific area. For example, overall you might like yourself and have high self-esteem. However, if you are poor and can't buy the clothes you want, you may have low specific self-

LIFT YOUR SPIRITS

From time to time we all feel a little down. Things aren't going your way. Sometimes it seems you can't shake this feeling. There is something you can do. Think about the blessings you have in your life. These might include your health, people you love and who love you, a roof over your head. The list goes on and on. Feeling gratitude lifts your attitude!

esteem about your appearance. A person with global self-esteem sees areas of low specific self-esteem as places to grow.

You can have high specific self-esteem in several roles and lack global self-esteem. Why? Because you don't value the roles in which you have specific self-esteem. You may say to yourself, "Sure, I'm a good parent, but so what?" If you don't value the areas in which you have high specific self-esteem, you still won't like yourself.

Or, you can lack global self-esteem because you don't have specific self-esteem in the roles that are most important to you. Take Andrea, for example. She is smart and liked by everyone. But Andrea doesn't like herself very much. Andrea wants to be a singer. In fact, the most important thing to her is to be a singer. Because Andrea is not a singer, no matter how good she feels about herself in some roles, overall she feels bad.

In what roles do you have specific self-esteem? What about your global self-esteem? How do you feel about yourself overall? Are you a likable, lovable, capable person?

SELF-ESTEEM AND JUDGMENT

The only way to like yourself is to accept yourself. You need to stop judging yourself. Judgment keeps you from accepting yourself and liking yourself. **Self-acceptance** is when you can say to yourself, "I am okay."

You learned about judgment almost from the day you were born. Your parents may have judged you more or less than other parents. The point is, you learned at an early age what was acceptable about you and what wasn't acceptable about you. You probably carry those same ideas today.

If you were told you were dumb as a child, you probably think of yourself as dumb. If you were told you were clumsy, you think of yourself as clumsy. If you were told you were pretty, you think of yourself as pretty. You judge yourself now the way others judged you then. No one else needs to do it anymore. Your Judge has taken over the job!

Do you know the difference between a fact and a judgment? A **fact** reports data. Facts are not emotional. Facts do not judge. A fact does not say that the data is good, bad, right, or wrong. A **judgment**, however, assigns value. A judgment says something is good or bad, okay or not okay. Let's look at a couple of examples.

Lydia is a poor reader. JUDGMENT
Lydia reads at the fourth grade level. FACT
Nobody likes me. JUDGMENT
My next door neighbor, Susan, doesn't speak when she sees me. FACT

What a difference! One sentence uses facts to describe the situation. The other sentence makes a judgment about the situation. Which one do you think will build your self-esteem? You're right! The fact, not the judgment. As long as you judge yourself, you will also judge others.

✔ CHECKPOINT 2-3

YOUR GOAL:
Get 5 or more answers correct.

Read each of the following statements. Decide if each statement is a fact or a judgment. Write the word *Fact* or *Judgment* in the space provided. An example has been completed for you. Give yourself one point for each correct answer.

- <u>Judgment</u>   I'm fat.

1. _____   I'm no good at school.

2. _____   I lose everything.

3. _____   I have a scar on my right cheek.

4. _____   I can remember up to three things without writing them down.

5. _____   On weekends I like to relax and do nothing for a few hours.

6. _____   I'm lazy.

☞ *Check your work. Record your score.*

You will discover that liking yourself is easier if you stop judging yourself and just tell the facts. You will find you can accept yourself. Over the next couple of days, listen to what you say to yourself. See if you can notice when you judge yourself.

Listen for your inner Judge. If you can catch the Judge starting to put you down, you can stop the judgments.

When you stop judging and start accepting, your self-esteem will stop acting like a yo-yo. Your self-esteem will be more even each day.

WHAT YOU HAVE LEARNED

Your self-esteem is affected by the skills you have, your inner Judge, and how other people treat you. Any of these can make your self-esteem go up or down. You play some roles in your life you feel good about. You have specific self-esteem in these roles. If you like yourself overall, you have global self-esteem. One way you can keep your self-esteem from being like a yo-yo is to use facts instead of judgments. As you accept yourself, you will build your self-esteem.

ACTIVITY 2-1 **YOUR GOAL:** Get 5 or more answers correct.

Match the definitions listed to the correct word or phrase. Write the correct answer in the space provided. An example has been completed for you. Give yourself one point for each correct answer.

a. global self-esteem   b. acceptance
c. judgment   d. self-esteem
e. Judge   f. specific self-esteem
g. fact   h. opinion

-   __d__   How you feel about yourself.

1. _____ An inner voice that criticizes you.

2. _____ Assigns value; decides if something is right or wrong.

3. _____ How you feel about yourself in general.

4. _____ How you feel about yourself in a role; for example, parenting.

5. _____ Data, or a description of a situation.

6. _____ The opposite of judgment.

☞ *Check your work. Record your score.*

ACTIVITY 2-2 **YOUR GOAL:** Get 8 or more answers correct.

Read the following list. Decide which ones would help build your self-esteem. In the space provided, write *yes* if the item would build self-esteem. Write *no* if it would not. An example has been completed for you. Give yourself one point for each correct answer.

-   __no__   Use "should" when you talk to yourself or others.
1. _____ Learn new skills.
2. _____ Judge yourself.
3. _____ Spend time with people who are negative.
4. _____ Compliment yourself when you do something well.
5. _____ Believe in yourself.
6. _____ Criticize yourself.
7. _____ Choose friends who encourage you.
8. _____ Accept yourself as you are.
9. _____ Say things to yourself like, "You can do it!"
10. _____ Look for your mistakes.

☞ *Check your work. Record your score.*

UNIT 3
WHERE DOES SELF-ESTEEM COME FROM?

WHAT YOU WILL LEARN

When you finish this unit, you will be able to:

- Describe how your childhood affects your self-esteem.
- Identify four masks you may wear.

If you have ever been around a newborn baby, you know that the first feeling is one of awe. You can't help but be moved by the miracle of life. In the first few days, most parents see their baby as perfect and give the child unconditional love. **Unconditional love** is loving someone or being loved no matter what you do, say, feel, or think. Parents don't expect the baby to do anything. They love the baby just because he/she is alive.

Unconditional love is soon replaced with conditional love. **Conditional love** is loving someone or being loved *if* certain conditions are met. For example, the child is loved *if* he/she behaves in a certain way. You love him *if* he eats his dinner, *if* she picks up her toys, *if* he shares with other children, *if* she is quiet when you are on the phone. It is no longer enough for the child to be. You expect the child to do what you want. Judgment begins.

CHILDHOOD AND YOUR SELF-ESTEEM

Therefore, as a child you begin to learn that you are okay— *if.* Parents don't mean to hurt you or your self-esteem. They do the best they can with what they know. Sometimes when they think they are teaching you, they are really judging you.

Those early judgments become your Judge. That's why today, as an adult, you can still hear the words of your mother, father, or whoever raised you. Even if they are dead, the Judge repeats their words to you.

LIFT YOUR SPIRITS

Judging yourself and others is so easy. Instead of judging, you want to observe and notice differences. A phrase you might say to yourself is, "I'm doing the best I can." This will help you avoid blaming. You can use a similar phrase when someone else doesn't do things your way. Say to yourself, "She's doing the best she can." That simple phrase will save you lots of upset feelings.

Your **personal history** is everything that has happened in your life up until today. This history includes your experiences as a child, everything that has happened to you, and the things that were said to you. Each person has a different personal history. That is part of what makes you unique as a human being. No one else on the planet is exactly like you!

How You Were Judged

Because you are unique, you are different from your parents in some ways. Very often when someone is different we judge the difference. We see the difference as good or bad, better or worse. For example, your parents might have loved sports. Perhaps they watched sports on TV, or listened to games on the radio. Maybe you didn't like sports. Perhaps you preferred to listen to music.

Your parents could handle this difference in two ways. They could say, "What's wrong with you that you're off in your room listening to music when the game is on?!" This is a judgment that hurts your self-esteem. Your **preference**, or your personal choice, is not accepted. Your preference is judged as bad, and you feel wrong or not okay. You might think to yourself, "What's wrong with me that I don't like sports?"

A more positive way to handle the difference would be for your parents to say, "We're going to watch the game. Would you like to watch it with us, or would you prefer to do something else?" They give you permission to be different. You learn that you are unique and that that is okay.

Now, as an adult, you may judge yourself the way you were judged as a child. Here comes the Judge, again! You will feel better about yourself if you change your judgments into preferences.

Let's see how this works. If you judge yourself by saying, "I should make more money," you will feel bad about yourself. If you change the words you say to yourself, you will feel different. Try saying, "I would prefer to make more money." Now you aren't attacking yourself.

You can also change a judgment into a goal by using the words "I want." Instead of saying "I should make more money," you would say, "I want to make more money." The *should* makes you feel as if there is something wrong with you because you aren't making more money. "I want to make more money," gets you to start thinking about how you could do it.

✔ CHECKPOINT 3-1

YOUR GOAL:
Get 5 or more answers correct.

Read each of the following judgments. Change each to either a preference or a goal as directed. An example has been completed for you. Give yourself one point for each correct answer.

- I should lose weight.

  PREFERENCE: _____ I would prefer to weigh less. _____

1. I should quit smoking.

   GOAL: _____

2. I should read better.

   GOAL: _____

3. I shouldn't have made a mistake.

   PREFERENCE: _____

4. The bus should be on time.

   PREFERENCE: _____

5. I should keep the house cleaner.

   PREFERENCE: _____

6. I should have more friends.

   GOAL: _____

☞ *Check your work. Record your score.*

Steppingstones Or Walls?

All of us have felt some pain growing up. Growing from childhood to adulthood can be difficult. Although your parents did the best they could, they may not have given you what you needed. There is no need for you to blame them now. You want to *understand* your personal history, not judge it. Understanding your history will help you understand yourself.

Then, you want to grow beyond your personal history. You want to use your past as a steppingstone to the future. You do not want to use your past to build walls.

Your mind is like a movie camera. It takes pictures of everything that happens to you. Some of these pictures are stored away, and you forget you have them. But some of the pictures you watch over and over again on the movie screen in your mind. Some of these movies make you feel good, as in Illustration 3-1. You might watch the movie of a good time you shared with a friend. Maybe you watch the movie of being read to as a child. Perhaps the movie is of a special holiday that you enjoyed.

Illustration 3-1

The Good Times

Other movies don't make you feel good. These movies make you feel scared, or inadequate, or embarrassed, or sad. These movies are of unpleasant things that happened to you. Perhaps you were physically abused growing up. Maybe you are an incest victim. You might have had an alcoholic parent. Or, you may have grown up in foster homes because your parents couldn't care for you.

Each person has positive and negative movies. Sometimes an event will trigger one of your movies. Take a minute now to think of one of your positive movies.

Watching the movies in your mind is how you keep a memory alive. And like any good movie, if it is vivid, with lots of detail, you will feel what you see in the movie. In other words, if you remember a funny time, you may find yourself laughing at the memory. If you remember a scary time, you may feel afraid again.

If you choose to watch the negative movies again and again, you will keep feeling the same bad feelings you had as a child. If

LIFT YOUR SPIRITS

"For men and women are not only themselves; they are also the region in which they were born, the city apartment or farm in which they learned to walk, the games they played as children, the old wive's tales they overheard, the food they ate, the school they attended, the sports they followed, the poems they read, and the God they believed in."

W. Somerset Maugham

The Razor's Edge

you watch the positive movies, you will find yourself feeling good. It is your choice. Which movies do you watch?

Some people only watch the negative movies. After years of reruns, they create walls that keep other people out. They won't run the risk of being hurt by someone new. They watch their movies and feel hurt again and again by the same players.

They use their movies as an excuse for not trying anything new. What difference would it make? they think. They already know the ending from the movies they are watching. These people do not learn from their painful experiences. They become trapped by them. They end up feeling bad about themselves.

To stop being hurt by the negative movies, you need to learn how to have a positive focus. A **positive focus** is looking for what is positive in a situation and focusing on that. You don't lie to yourself and say you had a wonderful childhood if you didn't. Instead you look for what you learned about yourself as a result of the experience. You look for how you are a better person today because of what you experienced. Let's look at a couple of examples of a positive focus in a difficult situation.

Situation: I was criticized for everything I did as a child.
Positive focus: Now as an adult I look for what other people do right, instead of what they do wrong. I give others compliments and help them feel good about themselves.

Situation: I grew up with an alcoholic parent that I couldn't count on, and I was often disappointed.
Positive focus: People can count on me. If I say I'm going to do something, I follow through, even if I don't always feel like it.

Situation: I never felt my parents liked me or cared about me. They were often away from home, and I spent lots of time alone.
Positive focus: I am an independent person. I like other people, but I know I can take care of myself. I don't have to have other people around me to feel okay about myself.

Anyone in any of these three situations easily could have built walls as a result of the difficult early experiences. The person who was criticized could have grown up to attack and criticize others. The person from an alcoholic family could have coped by drinking. And the person who was alone could have withdrawn and become depressed.

CHECKPOINT 3-2

YOUR GOAL:
Get 5 or more answers correct.

Read each of the following situations. Decide if the person used an experience as a steppingstone or to build a wall. In the space provided, write the word *Steppingstone* or *Wall*. Give yourself one point for each correct answer. An example has been completed for you.

●   <u>Wall</u>   I was compared with my older brother who got A's in school. School was hard for me, and I quit before I graduated. I try to avoid people who went to college.

1. _____ I was told over and over that I was stupid. I never believed it. Now people at work say I am quick to catch on to new ideas.

2. _____ I learned children are to be seen and not heard. Now, as an adult, I don't speak up or tell people how I feel.

3. _____ No matter what I did, my parents told me I could do it better. I decided not doing anything is better than to risk doing it wrong.

4. _____ I was the last of six kids, and my parents didn't have time for me. I learned early that I would need to find other people to give me support and encouragement. Today, I make friends easily.

5. _____ My parents wanted things their way. They punished us if we disagreed, even when they were wrong. Today, I am a patient listener. I try to understand other people.

6. _____ My parents were very strict. I'm good at my job today because I can tell people the rules and I can enforce them.

☞ *Check your work. Record your score.*

The important point is that you cannot control what happens to you. But you can control how you react to what happens to you. You can act like a victim, and feel bad about yourself. Or you can take charge of how you react and feel good about yourself.

LIFT YOUR SPIRITS

PERSPECTIVE

*I don't have to
have it all or be it all*

*I don't need to
do it all or know it all.*

*What I do need is
to know who I am,
know what I want,
know what makes me happy
and know how
to get my needs met.*

*If I can do that successfully,
all the rest will fall into place.*

—Leslie Charles, President

TRAININGWORKS, inc.

Leslie Charles received her G.E.D. at age 29, and is now President of her own training firm that serves companies across the United States.

THE MASKS WE WEAR

If you don't like yourself, you may try to hide this fact from other people. One way to do that is to wear a mask, as in Illustration 3-2. You pretend that you like yourself. Most of the time, other people can tell when you wear a mask. They would rather see the real you.

Wearing a mask is hard on you for two reasons. First, you are always acting. You try to be someone you are not. Acting is a lot of work and can cause stress. Second, if people like your mask self, then you still feel bad about yourself. Why? Because they like who you pretend you are — not who you really are.

Illustration 3-2

The Masks We
Wear

If you can drop your mask and be yourself, you will like yourself better. Without the mask, you can focus on changing the parts of yourself you don't like, instead of trying to hide them.

People wear different masks. You may change your mask to fit a new situation. Do you wear any of these masks?

1. **Macho/Tough Mask** - Men wear this mask more than women, but either sex can act tough. These people brag about how they got into a fight, or how they used words to hurt someone. They often use curse words and do not show any feelings except anger. People who wear this mask really feel scared on the inside. They hide how they feel with the Tough/Macho Mask. People who are really strong don't need to brag about it. Other people know if you are strong. The louder you try to convince others about how tough you are, the more they know the real truth. People who wear this mask can sometimes be dangerous because they will go to extremes to try to "prove" how tough they are.

2. **I'm the Greatest Mask** - These people can't stop talking about themselves. They brag about everything. They try to impress you with who they know, the things they have, or how well they are doing. They often stretch the truth to try to impress you. They don't realize that you can see through their tall tales. They like to be the first to know things. All of this is a cover for the fact that inside they don't feel good about themselves. They don't feel okay. They try to convince themselves that they are okay by trying to convince others to like them. It is tiring to be around someone who is constantly telling you how wonderful he or she is. People who wear this mask may drive others away rather than draw them closer.

3. **Blaming and Complaining Mask** - Have you been around people who begin and end each conversation with how awful things are? They want to tell you how they are being cheated by their boss, mistreated by their friends, or ignored by their family. In every situation, something goes wrong. They believe nothing will ever work out for them. All of this complaining is to try and get you to do something for them. They can't take any positive action for themselves. They think that the only reason anyone would spend time with them is because of their problems. They don't realize that most people do not want to be around someone who only has problems. Complaining drives others away. It does not attract friends.

4. **Mr. Nice Guy/Ms. Nice Gal Mask** - At first you want to be with these people. They are so nice, friendly, and helpful. You feel good to know them. But over time, you may start to distrust them. How can anyone always be nice? How can a person never have any negative feelings? Is there such a thing as a perfect person? People who wear this mask try to make sure there is no possible reason for you not to like them. This is how they hide the fact that they don't like themselves. They think that if they are always nice they will be liked. This mask prevents them from being human. We like to be around people who, like us, are human. Humans do make mistakes. We are moody sometimes. The person who is always nice doesn't seem real. They may be used by others because they don't say "No."

Do you know people who wear these masks? Which masks do you wear? When you have high self-esteem, you express your real self. You know that your real self is okay. You can be yourself.

✔ ## CHECKPOINT 3-3

YOUR GOAL:
Get 4 answers correct.

Read each of the following situations and decide which mask is being described. Write your answer in the space provided. An example has been completed for you. Give yourself one point for each correct answer.

● If you ever needed a ride somewhere, you could count on George. He would go out of his way for you. Or, if you were short of money before pay day, he would loan you money. He's the kind of guy you can depend on.

Mr. Nice Guy
_____

1. These people seem to always get their way. They don't
    hesitate to yell if things aren't the way they want them.
    They can scare you sometimes because they don't seem to
    have any feelings.

    _____

2. This woman doesn't believe anyone would pay attention
    to her. To get attention, she complains a lot. Her land-
    lord doesn't make repairs, her kids have problems in
    school, she feels sick. The complaints never stop.

    _____

3. You would think this man owned the company where he
    works. To listen to him talk, nothing would get done
    without him. He's always meeting with the big shots. He
    acts like he knows everybody. It's hard to believe all the
    great things he tells you about himself.

    _____

4. This woman has a heart of gold. She doesn't know the
    word "no." She would give you her last dollar. She seems
    so concerned about others it is sometimes hard to believe
    she is for real.

    _____

☞ *Check your work. Record your score.*

WHAT YOU HAVE LEARNED

Your childhood has an effect on your self-esteem. Even though
your parents did the best they could, they may not have given you
what you needed. Differences between you and your parents
may have been judged. As an adult, you want to look for the
positive in your childhood experiences. You want to use those
experiences as steppingstones to a better future. Sometimes
people try to hide feelings of low self-esteem behind a mask of
toughness, I'm great, blaming, or being nice. Most people can
see through these masks. You'll like yourself more when you stop
wearing masks.

ACTIVITY 3-1 **YOUR GOAL:** Get 8 or more answers correct.

Read each of the following statements. Put a *T* in the space provided if a statement is true. Put an *F* if the statement is false. An example has been completed for you. Give yourself one point for each correct answer.

-    __T__   Unconditional love means you are loved no matter what you do, how you feel, or what you think.

1. _____ Most children grow up with conditional love.

2. _____ If you are different from another person, you may be judged.

3. _____ Judgment leads to high self-esteem.

4. _____ If you say, "I prefer. . . ," you are judging.

5. _____ If you had an unhappy childhood, you can never have high self-esteem.

6. _____ You can control how you react to a situation, even if you can't control what happens.

7. _____ Some people wear masks to hide the fact that they don't like themselves.

8. _____ If you act tough, other people will be impressed and like you.

9. _____ Global self-esteem is all of the things that have happened to you in your life.

10. _____ If unpleasant things happened to you while you were growing up, you can never like yourself.

☞ *Check your work. Record your score.*

ACTIVITY 3-2   YOUR GOAL: Get 4 or more answers correct.

Answer each of the following questions in the space provided. An example has been completed for you. Give yourself one point for each correct answer.

● Why do most parents judge their children?

   They don't know any better.

1. How does remembering a happy or sad time affect you today?

2. How can you change a judgment to something more positive?

3. How can a positive focus change how you feel about negative things that happened to you?

4. What is meant by "You can't control what happens to you, but you can control your reaction?"

5. What are the two disadvantages of wearing a mask?

☞ *Check your work. Record your score.*

PART TWO
THE CAUSES OF LOW SELF-ESTEEM

UNIT 4
NEGATIVE THINKING

UNIT 5
MISTAKEN BELIEFS

UNIT 6
COMPARISONS AND YOUR SELF-ESTEEM

UNIT 7
PERFECTIONISM

UNIT 4
NEGATIVE THINKING

WHAT YOU WILL LEARN

When you finish this unit, you will be able to:

- Change your shoulds to more positive self-talk.
- Change overgeneralizations to facts.
- Stop using labels to describe yourself.
- Replace fortune telling with goal setting.
- Identify examples of catastrophizing.

All day long you talk to yourself. You remind yourself to pick up milk at the store. You plan what you will do over the weekend. You rehearse what you will say to your boss. You remember things that happened in the past. These conversations that you have with yourself are called **self-talk**. Everyone does it.

Some people talk positively to themselves. Other people talk negatively to themselves. If your self-talk is negative, you will have low self-esteem. If your self-talk is positive, you will have high self-esteem.

In this unit you will learn how to tell if your self-talk is positive or negative. If it is negative, you will learn how to change it to positive self-talk.

SHOULD STATEMENTS

Of all the ways that you can talk negatively to yourself, should statements are the most damaging. Other words that have the same effect are *ought*, *must*, and *have to*. These words judge you. They make you feel guilty and not okay. They are the words of the Judge. They come from other people's expectations.

There are three types of shoulds: Having, Doing, and Being. Some examples of each kind follow.

Having Shoulds ▬▬▬▬▬▬▬▬▬▬▬▬▬▬

You tell yourself that you should have certain things. If you have those things, you will be okay. Maybe you can show others that you are successful. For example:

    You should have a good job.
    You should have a nice car.
    You should have a color TV.

Doing Shoulds ▬▬▬▬▬▬▬▬▬▬▬▬▬▬

You tell yourself that you should do certain things to be accepted by others. Or, maybe you tell yourself that if you were a good person you would do these things. For example:

    You should act your age.
    You should go to school.
    You should spend time with your children.

Being Shoulds ▬▬▬▬▬▬▬▬▬▬▬▬▬▬

You tell yourself what traits you need to be okay. You expect yourself to have these qualities in all situations. For example:

    You should be nice.
    You should be perfect.
    You should be strong.

Now think about the shoulds in your life. Make a list of them in the space provided. Then go through the list and for each should decide if it is a Having, Doing, or Being should.

<u>My Shoulds</u>	<u>Kind of Should</u>
_____	_____
_____	_____
_____	_____
_____	_____

If you have lots of shoulds in your life, they control you. You spend your time doing what you should do instead of what you want to do. That's why you need to let go of your shoulds. If you could stop using the words *should, ought, must,* and *have to* tomorrow, you would instantly feel better about yourself.

By now, using shoulds when you talk to yourself has become a habit. Habits take work to change. Changing negative self-talk to positive self-talk will take work. But you can make a change! Here's how. When you catch yourself saying *should, ought, must,* or *have to,* change to one of these words:

      choose to   consider
      prefer   need
      want   wish

None of these words are judgmental. Using them will not lower your self-esteem.

✔ CHECKPOINT 4-1

YOUR GOAL:
Get 5 or more answers correct.

Read each of the following should statements. Rewrite each statement so it is no longer a should statement. Use words from the list below to rewrite the statements. An example has been completed for you. Give yourself one point for each correct answer.

choose to	consider	prefer
need	want	wish

● I should study more.

   <u>I want to study more.</u>

1. I shouldn't make a mistake.

   _____

2. I should be on time.

   _____

3. I should read better.

   _____

4. I should have called first.

   _____

5. I shouldn't loan Mark money.

   _____

6. I should be more understanding.

   _____

☞ *Check your work. Record your score.*

OVERGENERALIZATION

Overgeneralization is when you take one experience and turn it into a rule about life. For example, you apply for a job, and you aren't chosen. You could overgeneralize by saying, "I'll never find a job."

Being passed over for one job does not mean you will not find a job. The overgeneralization, though, just about guarantees you won't find a job. If you believe what you're telling yourself, you'll decide there is no point in trying. You will make your overgeneralization come true by your own actions.

There are several words that are a clue that you are overgeneralizing. They are:

always	all
never	every
everybody	none
nobody	

To turn this type of negative thinking into positive thinking, you need to state only the facts to yourself. No judgment of the facts! Imagine that you and a friend have a fight. Afterwards you can make it worse if you overgeneralize and tell yourself, "Nobody likes me." That isn't even true! But you can make yourself believe it and feel bad.

A better way to talk to yourself is to tell yourself the facts. You could say, "My friend and I had a fight, and he is mad at me now." This statement describes reality. There is no judgment. You can live with the truth. The overgeneralization makes you feel bad about yourself.

CHECKPOINT 4-2

YOUR GOAL: Get 8 or more answers correct.

Read each of the following statements. Underline the clue word or words that tell you the statements are overgeneralizations. Two statements have more than one overgeneralization clue word. An example has been completed for you. Give yourself one point for each correct answer.

- I'll <u>never</u> be able to trust anyone again.
1. None of my bosses have been any good.
2. I always hit every red light.
3. Nobody helps me.
4. Every time I ride the bus, all the seats are taken.
5. Everybody in the class understands this except me.
6. Sara is never on time.
7. All the good jobs are gone.
8. No one works as hard as I do.

☞ *Check your work. Record your score.*

LABELING - YOU DO IT TO YOURSELF

You're twisting reality out of shape again! When you **label**, you describe yourself, others, or situations in a negative way, as in Illustration 4-1. For example, if you make a mistake, you might label yourself by saying, "What a stupid thing to do."

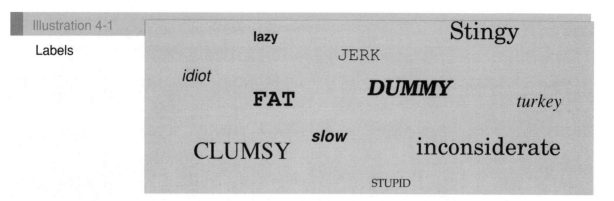

Illustration 4-1

Labels

If someone else makes the mistake, you might label him or her by saying, "What can you expect from a dummy?" If you feel unhappy in a situation you might say, "This is a mess because of those crooked politicians."

In each of the preceding examples, you are using a negative word or phrase. You present the situation as if it is hopeless, and you are powerless to change it. You also upset yourself with the negative labels. How can you feel high self-esteem if you are calling yourself names?

You change labeling the same way you change overgeneralization. You need to describe reality without judging it. Labeling is one more way that you judge. If you make a mistake, you say to yourself, "I made a mistake. How can I fix it?" There is no need to label yourself.

If someone else makes a mistake, you can tell them about it. For example, if the store clerk gives you the wrong change you can say, "You gave me the wrong change." You don't need to label him or her.

Are you beginning to see how many of your bad feelings about yourself come from the way you talk to yourself?

LIFT YOUR SPIRITS

Make a list of some of the negative things you say to yourself. Then rewrite these statements so that they are positive instead of negative. The next time you notice yourself saying the negative statement, change it to the positive one. If you do this for just one month, you will be surprised at how much better you feel about yourself.

FORTUNE TELLING

It would be nice if you could look into a crystal ball and know the future, as in Illustration 4-2. You can't do that, though. Some people act as if they can predict the future. And what they see is usually negative.

Illustration 4-2

Fortune Telling

Fortune telling is predicting the future. It is usually negative. If you use fortune telling, then you may recognize some of these phrases:

Why try? You'll never succeed.

You won't be invited to the party.

They won't hire you for the job.

You don't know enough to pass the test.

Each of these phrases predicts the future. And they don't predict a positive future. If you say these types of statements to yourself often enough, they tend to come true.

If you keep telling yourself you won't get hired for the job you want, you probably won't. Even though you are disappointed when you don't get hired, at least you can say you were right! "See, I told you I wouldn't get hired."

Fortune telling is a vicious circle that keeps you from having high self-esteem. How do you break this habit? Instead of predicting the worst, start planning for what you want. Set a goal for yourself. If you want to pass a test at school, set a goal to get a passing grade. Then ask yourself what you need to do to make that goal come true. Imagine yourself meeting your goal.

LIFT YOUR SPIRITS

Sit down and write yourself a love letter. Tell yourself all the things you like about yourself. Compliment yourself on the things you do well. On days when you feel down, read your love letter to yourself.

Fortune telling and goal setting are very similar *except* that with goals you focus on what you want instead of what you don't want. Any time you notice yourself starting to feel self-doubt, watch out for fortune telling. Avoiding fortune telling is one way to keep your self-esteem high.

CATASTROPHIZING

Catastrophizing is making a mountain out of a mole hill. You turn a headache into a brain tumor. You catastrophize by imagining, "What if. . ." For example, if you make an error at work, you might say to yourself, "What if they fire me?" You blow things out of proportion when you catastrophize. Here are several more examples:

You are driving alone at night and think, "What if I have a flat tire?"

While you study for a test, you think to yourself, "What if I fail?"

You see a TV show about kids and drugs and think, "What if my child is addicted to drugs?"

When you catastrophize, you live in a state of fear. You worry a lot. This needless fear can stop you from doing things that would help you grow. You aren't building your self-esteem.

CHECKPOINT 4-3

YOUR GOAL:
Get 4 or more aswers correct.

Read each of the following statements. They are each an example of labeling, fortune telling, or catastrophizing. Write which type of negative thinking each statement is in the space provided. An example has been completed for you. Give yourself one point for each correct answer.

- Some jerk worked on my car, and it still doesn't run right.

    _____labeling_____

1. Why ask my boss for the day off? I know he won't give it to me.

    _____

2. If I was a brown-noser, I'd get a raise, too.

    _____

3. You smell gas and think, "What if the house blows up? Where will we live then?"

    _____

4. The landlord won't fix the front step, so why bother telling him about it?

    _____

5. I'm a worthless excuse for a parent.

    _____

6. What if this assignment isn't perfect, and I flunk out of school?

    _____

☞ *Check your work. Record your score.*

The secret to avoiding negative self-talk is to describe reality. Don't judge it. Judgment kills your self-esteem. Try to tell the truth about what you see and observe. Avoid giving your opinion if it will be a judgment. Later in this book you will learn more ways to replace your negative self-talk with positive self-talk.

It will not be easy to change your habits of negative self-talk. But you can do it!   Don't criticize yourself when you notice yourself in an old habit.   Instead, congratulate yourself for noticing the negative self-talk. You can't change something until you are aware of it. As you practice the ideas in this unit, you will notice that less and less of your self-talk is negative.

LIFT YOUR SPIRITS

One way to break the negative thinking habit is to do something called <u>Thought Stopping.</u> When you notice a negative thought, tell yourself STOP! and picture a red stop sign. You will stop the negative thought. Then change your negative thought into one that is positive. Use the suggestions in this unit to turn a negative thought into a positive one.

WHAT YOU HAVE LEARNED

You talk to yourself all day long. Some of what you say is positive, and some of what you say is negative. The negative self-talk includes shoulds, overgeneralizations, labeling, fortune telling, and catastrophizing. All of these negative thoughts are judgments of you. They lower your self-esteem. You want to observe and describe reality instead of judging it with these negative thoughts.

ACTIVITY 4-1 YOUR GOAL: Get 8 or more answers correct.

Read each of the following statements. Write *T* if a statement is true in the space provided. Write *F* if the statement is false. An example has been completed for you. Give yourself one point for each correct answer.

- ●   _T_   You talk to yourself all day long.
- 1. _____ Overgeneralization is the most damaging type of self-talk.
- 2. _____ There are three types of shoulds — wishing, wanting, and having.
- 3. _____ Negative self-talk is judgmental.
- 4. _____ If you say words like never, always, no one, or everybody, you are overgeneralizing.
- 5. _____ You can change negative self-talk to positive self-talk.
- 6. _____ You can change your shoulds by using the words choose, prefer, want, need, consider, or wish.
- 7. _____ Negative self-talk is a habit that can be changed.
- 8. _____ Fortune telling and goal setting are very similar.
- 9. _____ Fortune telling is when you use the words *should*, *ought*, *must*, or *have to*.
- 10. _____ Your self-talk affects how you feel about yourself.

☞ *Check your work. Record your score.*

ACTIVITY 4-2 YOUR GOAL: Get 10 or more answers correct..

Read the following paragraph. Underline any negative thought. Write the type of negative thought above the word or phrase. Give yourself one point for each word or phrase that is correctly underlined. Give yourself another point if you correctly stated the type of negative thought.

    I got up late this morning. I should have gone to bed earlier. The bus is never on time, so it really didn't matter. All the way to school I worried about my math test. "What if I fail it? What if I flunk the course?" I'm a real dummy when it comes to math. I've never understood fractions, and I probably never will.

☞ *Check your work. Record your score.*

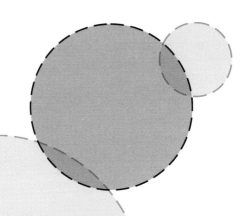

UNIT 5
MISTAKEN BELIEFS

WHAT YOU WILL LEARN

When you finish this unit, you will be able to:

- Identify how beliefs create feelings.
- Separate irrational from affirming beliefs.
- Identify the expectation behind angry or upset feelings.

Your self-talk comes from your beliefs. You have certain ideas about who you are, the way the world works, and the way other people are. These ideas all fit together to make your belief system about the world. You might think of it as being a road map that you have created. It is your map of the way you think things are.

You put your road map together based on what you learned as a child. Some parts of your map are correct. But many parts of your map are not correct. Unless someone can show you where your map is wrong, you will continue to believe and act as if it is true. If your map is incorrect, you may follow it and find that it doesn't take you where you want to go. In this unit you will have a chance to think about your beliefs, and decide if they are getting you where you want to go in your life.

 YOUR BELIEFS CREATE YOUR FEELINGS

A psychologist named Albert Ellis developed a model to help people understand the power of beliefs. His model is shown in Illustration 5-1.

Illustration 5-1	A ⟶ B ⟶ C ⟶ D
Model of Belief System	Activating event Belief Consequential Doing (Situation) Feeling

A stands for *Activating event*. You can think of this as a situation. Ellis said that situations by themselves are neither positive nor negative. They simply are.

For example, a divorce isn't positive or negative. It is. Getting a raise isn't positive or negative. It is. Having an argument with your best friend isn't positive or negative. It is. In other words, Ellis does not judge any situation.

The *B* of the model stands for *Beliefs*. Each person has a set of beliefs he or she uses to make sense of the world. Your beliefs are part of your roadmap. Different people may have different beliefs about the same Activating event or situation.

For example, Marta might believe divorce is wrong. Mark might believe divorce is okay in certain situations, such as if one spouse is battering the other one. Mildred might believe divorce is okay if the two people involved want the divorce. Who is right? They are each right. They each have their own beliefs about the situation.

People can even have different beliefs about getting a raise! M. C. could believe a raise will give him more money to support the family. Nelia could believe the raise would only cause her to pay more taxes.

Knowing your beliefs leads to *C* in the model. The *C* stands for *Consequential feelings*. In other words, how you feel in a situation is a result of what you believe about the situation. How you feel is not a result of the situation.

Marta might feel hurt, angry, and guilty if her partner wanted a divorce. Mildred would feel differently about a divorce. She might feel sad that the relationship didn't work, but not angry or guilty because she was going through a divorce. Marta and Mildred's feelings are different because they have different beliefs about divorce.

M. C. would feel excited about extra money for his family. Because Nelia believes the extra money will all go to the government, she would feel differently. Instead of feeling excited, Nelia might feel frustrated that she can't get ahead. Getting a raise is not what caused M. C.'s excitement and Nelia's frustration. It was their beliefs about getting the raise that caused the feelings.

The last step of the model is *D* for *Doing*. Ellis says that our behavior (what we do) is a result of our beliefs and feelings. If Marta thinks divorce is wrong and feels upset about it, she might refuse to see an attorney. Mildred would be happy to see an attorney to work out a divorce that she and her husband thought was reasonable.

M. C. might thank his boss for the raise and take the family out to dinner to celebrate his new raise. Nelia wouldn't bother telling anyone about her raise because she wouldn't believe it was anything to get excited about.

Your beliefs are extremely powerful. It is not what happens in your life, but what you believe about what happens, that causes your feelings and actions. In other words, your beliefs about life shape your life.

✔ CHECKPOINT 5-1

YOUR GOAL:
Get 5 or more answers correct.

Read each of the paragraphs. Identify the Activating event, Belief, Consequential feeling, or Doing as directed. Write your answer in the space provided. An example has been completed for you. Give yourself one point for each correct answer.

● Chee has a test coming up at school. Chee believes he is a poor student and that studying won't help. Chee watches TV the night before his test. He does not study.
Activating event: ____test coming up_____

1. Marlene has a test coming up at school. She believes that she can do well in school if she is prepared. She starts studying the week before the test is scheduled.
Belief: _____

2. Frank's car won't start. Frank believes cars are impossible to understand. He feels overwhelmed when it won't start. He calls a tow truck to come start it.
Consequential feeling: _____

3. Nami's car won't start. She believes she can figure out most things that go wrong with a car. She feels confident she can get it going again. She lifts the hood and starts working on it.
Doing: _____

4. Juan's neighbor wants to borrow some tools. Juan believes that if you loan something it's the same as giving it away. He feels threatened and won't loan the tools.
Activating event: _____

5. Julie's neighbor wants to borrow some tools. She believes it is wrong to say "no" even though she wants to. She feels resentful. She loans the neighbor her tools.
Belief: _____

6. Rick's friend wants to borrow some money. Rick believes you have a right to say "no" if someone asks you for something. Rick feels comfortable saying no to his friend because he can't afford to loan the money. He tells his friend "no."
Consequential feeling: _____

☞ *Check your work. Record your score.*

IRRATIONAL BELIEFS

Ellis found that many people hold irrational beliefs. An **irrational belief** is a belief that isn't logical or true. Irrational beliefs cause you pain, frustration, disappointment, and anger. And they can cause low self-esteem. Here are some of the irrational beliefs Ellis lists. Are any of these beliefs your beliefs?

1. Everyone must love and approve of me.
2. I must be totally competent.
3. I must view things as awful if I am frustrated, treated unfairly, or rejected.
4. Unhappiness is caused by things outside my control.
5. If something is scary, I should worry about it as if it will happen.
6. It is easier to avoid problems than to face them.
7. My past is all-important and controls my future.

Let's look at one of these beliefs to understand what Ellis meant when he said they are irrational. The first one, "Everyone must love and approve of me," puts you in the impossible situation of trying to please others all the time. Often, to please one person is to displease another. Sometimes when you please others, you make yourself unhappy.

The belief suggests that if someone doesn't like you, something terrible will happen. The truth is, some people will like you

LIFT YOUR SPIRITS

Scientists have an easy way to catch monkeys. They go into a clearing and set out long-necked bottles. Inside the bottles, they put the kind of nuts the monkeys love. A few hours later they come back to the clearing and each bottle has a monkey attached! The monkeys put their arms into the long neck to get the nuts. They grab a handful and make a fist to hold them. Their fists won't come out of the narrow neck, and they won't let go of the nuts. They trap themselves, as shown in the illustration. Are you holding on to some beliefs that have you trapped?

no matter what you do. Some people won't like you, no matter what you do. And most people feel neutral about you.

If you try to please others all the time, you may do things that conflict with your values. Then you risk losing your self-respect. In Unit 1 we talked about how important self-respect is for high self-esteem.

For example, you might value honesty. Imagine that a friend asks you to lie for him about where he was last night. If you hold the belief that you need others' love and approval, you may lie to keep the approval of your friend. But you didn't make a decision based on your values, and you feel badly about yourself. You are in a no-win situation, and you are the loser.

CHECKPOINT 5-2

Read each of the following statements. Decide if they are irrational beliefs. Write *yes* if they are irrational in the spaces provided. Write *no* if they are not. An example has been completed for you. Give yourself one point for each correct answer.

-    __yes__   I must be totally competent.

1. _____   I must view things as awful if I am frustrated, treated unfairly, or rejected.

2. _____   You win some and you lose some.

3. _____   Unhappiness is caused by things outside my control.

4. _____   A penny saved is a penny earned.

5. _____   If something is scary, I should worry about it as if it will happen.

6. _____   Women earn less than men on the average.

7. _____   Life is fair.

8. _____   It is easier to avoid problems than to face them.

9. _____   My past is all-important and controls my future.

10. _____   The early bird catches the worm.

☞ *Check your work. Record your score.*

If you have an irrational belief, you need to replace it with one that is rational. One that affirms you. An **affirming belief** is one that makes you feel good about yourself. An irrational belief limits you. An affirming belief helps you grow.

You could change the belief that you need everyone's love and approval to one such as:

I prefer to have people's love and approval, although I know that isn't always possible, *or*

I will please myself which will please some people and displease others, *or*

I cannot please everyone all the time and that is okay.

Each of these statements is closer to reality. These affirming beliefs will not cause bad feelings. They will help you accept yourself and others. You will feel better about yourself if you replace irrational beliefs with more positive ones.

Your shoulds come from the beliefs you hold. As you change your beliefs, you will be able to let go of your shoulds. As you make these changes, you will like yourself more. You will take away some of the power of the Judge.

✔ CHECKPOINT 5-3

YOUR GOAL:
Get 7 or more answers correct.

Read through the following lists of beliefs. Decide if they are affirming or irrational beliefs. If they are affirming, write that word in the space provided. If they are irrational, write that word in the space provided. An example has been completed for you. Give yourself one point for each correct answer.

● Once I make a decision, I shouldn't ever change it.

    irrational

1. I don't deserve a happy home and a good job.

2. If I say what I feel, I will hurt other people's feelings.

3. Whatever I feel is okay. I can choose a positive way to express my feelings.

4. If I ask a question, I'll look stupid.

5. I make a mess of everything.

_____

6. I can solve my own problems.

_____

7. Other people know what is best for me.

_____

8. I am a lovable and capable person.

_____

☞ *Check your work. Record your score.*

EXPECTATIONS AND SELF-ESTEEM

There are two different types of expectations. One type is called the self-fulfilling prophecy. A **self-fulfilling prophecy** is when you believe something strongly, and it comes true. For example, if you have an overall belief that things will work out, they tend to. But if you have a basic belief that things will not go your way, then they don't seem to.

To build your self-esteem, you want to have a positive expectation that things will work out for the best. This is similar to having a positive attitude about life. You focus on what is positive instead of what is negative. Life has both positive and negative parts. Your job is to decide which part you will emphasize.

LIFT YOUR SPIRITS

Do something nice for yourself each day because you're worth it! For example, soak in a hot tub. Take time to enjoy a cup of coffee. Read a magazine you like. Call a friend. Take time out to watch the sunrise or sunset.

There is another type of expectation that will cause you to suffer. That is when you get a picture in your mind of how you want things, or how things "should" be. If reality doesn't match your picture, you feel upset or disappointed.

Let's look at an example. Imagine that you go out to start your car and the battery is dead. The engine won't even turn over. This is certainly an inconvenience. But how do most people respond? They get angry and upset. Why? Because they expect the car to start all the time (an overgeneralization). Wouldn't it be wonderful if no one ever had a car problem? That is not reality, however. The truth is, cars break down.

The expectation that the car will "always" start is the cause of the upset feeling. You could avoid being upset by changing the expectation to a preference. You might say to yourself, "I would prefer that the car start. I realize that there may be times when it doesn't start."

Your expectation is actually a hidden should. Another judgment. As you know, judgment is the enemy of your self-esteem. Every judgment that you release is a boost to your self-esteem.

When you notice yourself feeling upset or angry, ask yourself, "What was I expecting?" Then change that expectation, or should, into a preference. You will be amazed at the changes in how you feel.

CHECKPOINT 5-4

YOUR GOAL:
Get 4 or more answers correct.

- I was mad when Rafael was late.

  Expectation: ___Rafael should be on time.___

1. I was mad when it rained on the weekend.

   Expectation: _____

2. I was disappointed when Sue forgot my birthday.

   Expectation: _____

3. I was hurt when Tom didn't return my call.

   Expectation: _____

4. I was angry when the bus was late.

   Expectation: _____

5. I was upset when the washer broke down.

Expectation: _____

☞ *Check your work. Record your score.*

Do you see how powerful your beliefs are? They are the cause of your feelings. What you're doing today is because of your beliefs. You're reading this book because you believe it is possible to change. You're going to school because you believe an education can make a difference. If you had a different set of beliefs, you wouldn't be doing these things.

Take time to think about what your beliefs are. Your future depends on it!

WHAT YOU HAVE LEARNED

How you feel is a result of what you believe. If you change your thoughts, you can change your feelings. Some of your beliefs are irrational. Some of your beliefs aren't even true! When you hold on to these beliefs, you upset yourself. Beliefs form expectations. When your expectations aren't met, you may feel angry or upset. If you let go of your expectations, or judgments, you can control your feelings of anger and being upset.

ACTIVITY 5-1   **YOUR GOAL:** Get 8 or more answers correct.

Read each of the following statements. Put a *T* in the space provided if a statement is true or an *F* if it is false. An example has been completed for you. Give yourself one point for each correct answer.

-     __F__   All people have the same beliefs.

1.   _____   You learn many of your beliefs when you are a child.

2.   _____   You can change your beliefs.

3.   _____   Your feelings come from what you do.

4.   _____   Situations are neutral. Your beliefs about them make them good or bad.

5.   _____   Two people in the same situation will feel the same way.

6.   _____   Irrational beliefs cause many people to feel bad about themselves.

7.   _____   "I prefer not to make mistakes," is an example of an irrational belief.

8.   _____   The opposite of an irrational belief is a self-fulfilling belief.

9.   _____   Expectations can lead to disappointment.

10. _____   To build your self-esteem, change your expectations and shoulds to preferences.

☞ *Check your work. Record your score.*

ACTIVITY 5-2   YOUR GOAL: List 10 or more beliefs.

Write at least three of your beliefs in each of the following categories. You can write more if you want. Give yourself one point for each belief you list. Include all of your beliefs, whether they are irrational or affirming. An example has been completed for you.

- Relationships:

  Belief 1: _Everyone should have a partner._

  Belief 2: _There is one right person for me; I just need to find him/her._

  Belief 3: _It takes lots of work for a relationship to be happy._

1. Relationships

   Belief: _____

   Belief: _____

   Belief: _____

2. Happiness

   Belief: _____

   Belief: _____

   Belief: _____

3. School

   Belief: _____

   Belief: _____

   Belief: _____

4. Work

   Belief: _____

   Belief: _____

   Belief: _____

☞ *Check your work. Record your score.*

UNIT 6
COMPARISONS AND YOUR SELF-ESTEEM

WHAT YOU WILL LEARN

When you finish this unit, you will be able to:

- Explain how comparisons damage self-esteem.
- Change comparisons to observations.
- Identify what makes a person unique.

The biggest danger to your self-esteem is judgment. And judgment is something most people become expert at by a very young age. So far you have learned that you judge yourself with shoulds. There's more! You may also judge yourself with comparisons.

COMPARISONS DAMAGE SELF-ESTEEM

You were probably compared with a brother or sister, a neighbor, or some other child at an early age. You might have been smarter, or prettier, or faster than the other child. Or, you might have come out the loser in the comparison. Your parents didn't know they would damage your self-esteem when they compared you to other children. If they had known, they wouldn't have done it.

If you weren't compared by your parents, then you were certainly compared when you got to school. The purpose of a grading system is to give you feedback on what you've learned. Too often, grades are used to compare one student to another. That's why in this book you grade yourself. All the answers are in the back of the book. The purpose is for you to learn. The purpose is not to compare you to other students.

You may have compared your own children to each other without knowing it could lower their self-esteem. You probably only meant to point out the differences between them. Maybe you hoped to motivate one of them to do better. Instead, you judged them. You can compare *things*, but don't compare *people*.

LIFT YOUR SPIRITS

When a friend is having problems, you can listen and sympathize. Sometimes when you do this you are thinking to yourself, "I'm glad that's not happening to me." But that's comparing yourself. If the same friend has good news to share, what happens? Many times no one wants to listen. Why not? Comparing again. It is hard to celebrate another person's success if you think that makes you less in comparison. You can be a real friend to someone if you celebrate his or her successes. Let your friend know how happy you are to share the good news. Then watch your friendships grow!

Personal Comparisons

As you grow up, you carry into your adult life the things you learned as a child. If your mother compared you to your brother, you probably still compare yourself to your brother. If your father compared you to others, today you probably compare yourself to others. Perhaps you have put all of the comparisons into an "ideal" person that you compare yourself to, like a movie or rock star.

Comparing yourself to others is a habit that can be difficult to break. Here's why. Sometimes when you compare yourself with another person, you come out the winner! That feels good. You feel a boost to your self-esteem. Because it works, you do it again in another situation. You may be the winner again. You decide that comparing is a good thing.

Then it happens. You compare yourself to someone, and she or he comes out better. You come up short. You feel inadequate, defeated, perhaps even hopeless. You wonder what is wrong with you. Why don't you measure up? Your self-esteem suffers a serious blow. The effects of comparisons can be seen in Illustration 6-1.

So you try it again in another situation. Again you don't measure up. But if you keep comparing, a time will come when you are the winner again. You'll compare yourself to another person, and you will be smarter, or better looking, or nicer. The hurtful cycle starts all over again.

What do people compare? Anything and everything. See if you recognize any of these statements:

We're the same age, but he makes so much more money than I do.

Why can't I have a good relationship like she does?

He's better looking than I am.

She knows so much more about this than I do.

I'm not as smart as he is.

I'm a slow reader compared to her.

Have you said these things, or something similar, to yourself?

Illustration 6-1

Comparisons

✔ CHECKPOINT 6-1

YOUR GOAL:
Get 5 answers correct.

Read each of the following statements. Decide if a statement is a comparison or not. In the space provided, write *yes* if it is a comparison and *no* if it is not. An example has been completed for you. Give yourself one point for each correct answer.

-   __yes__   Carlotta is prettier than I am.

1. _____   Allen makes $6.50 an hour.

2. _____   Tamera has nicer clothes than I do.

3. _____   People like Travis better than me.

4. _____   I've never been married.

5. _____   Everybody but me is married.

☞ *Check your work. Record your score.*

Group Comparisons

Comparisons carried to an extreme can hurt more than your self-esteem. They can damage the self-esteem of whole groups of people. Comparisons are the basis of prejudice, and they can lead to hatred. Here's how it happens.

You don't like yourself. One way to feel better about yourself is to compare yourself to someone who is different. Then, instead

LIFT YOUR SPIRITS

Let other people's success inspire you! When you hear a story about someone who has achieved a goal, remind yourself that this is possible for you, too. Maybe not that same goal, but one of your own. If someone gets a better job, that lets you know it's possible for you to get a better job, too. If someone has a happy marriage, let that encourage you to develop a close relationship. Good news can spark your mind with what is possible.

of accepting the difference, you judge it. To boost your own self-esteem, you judge in your own favor.

For example, a man might compare himself to a woman and judge that he is better *because he is a man*. This gives him half the population that he can compare himself to and come out a winner. The comparison is no longer person to person. You become better than an entire group of people. When many men do this, sexism results.

Comparisons also happen along racial lines. For example, some white people have compared themselves to black people *based on skin color alone*, and decided they were "better." Again, self-esteem is based on judging a difference. Comparisons based on skin color cause racism.

Groups of people are compared based on their religious preferences, their sexual orientation, where they live, the type of work they do, how much money they earn, and so on. Some people can only feel good about themselves by hating others. The person who hates others tells the world just how insecure he or she really is.

How Comparisons Cause Low Self-Esteem

Some people who compare themselves to others and come out "ahead" still manage to feel bad about themselves. They feel bad because they tell themselves that even though they came out better in the comparison, what was being compared wasn't important. In other words, they are better at something that doesn't count for much. If they had come out poorly in the comparison, they would judge that comparison as very important. Let's look at an example to understand this better.

Imagine that you are at work, and you hear a manager yelling at an employee about a mistake, like in Illustration 6-2. You might think to yourself, "Boy, I'm much nicer than he is." But in the next breath you might add, "Yeah, and see where it's got me — nowhere." You compared yourself, and you came out better. Then, you quickly devalued yourself by saying it didn't matter because being nice isn't important.

Illustration 6-2

Comparing Actions

You could run this scene a different way and get the same outcome. This time when you hear the manager yelling, you think to yourself, "Boy, he sure knows how to stand up for himself. I can't do that at all. If I could, my life would be so much better." In this example, you did not come out ahead in the comparison, and you decided that this quality was extremely important.

In these examples, no matter how you came out in the comparison, you managed to turn it into a negative for your self-esteem. As the saying goes, "You can't win for losing." Comparisons and high self-esteem just don't mix.

CHECKPOINT 6-2

YOUR GOAL:
Get 8 or more answers correct.

Read each of the following statements. If a statement is true, put a *T* in the space provided. If it is false, put an *F* in the space provided. An example has been completed for you. Give yourself one point for each correct answer.

●   <u>F</u>   Comparisons build self-esteem.

1.   <u>   </u>   Prejudice is caused by comparing and judging differences.

2.   <u>   </u>   Most people were judged as children.

3.   <u>   </u>   Some comparisons are good.

4. _____   Sometimes you feel better about yourself if you compare yourself to someone else.

5. _____   All comparisons are based on how smart you are.

6. _____   When you compare yourself to others, you judge yourself.

7. _____   You can motivate people to do better if you compare them to others.

8. _____   Comparing yourself to others is a habit you can break.

9. _____   You can compare yourself to someone, come out better, and still feel bad.

10. _____   If what is compared is important to you and you come out "ahead," you would feel bad about yourself.

☞ *Check your work. Record your score.*

CHANGE COMPARISONS TO OBSERVATIONS

How can you break the comparison habit? Change your comparisons to observations. Notice differences; don't judge them. Describe differences; don't compare them.

Let's look at some examples of how observation is different from comparison:

Comparison: Hiro is smarter than I am.
Observation: Hiro got an A on his math test.

Comparison: Juanell has more friends than I do.
Observation: There were 30 people at Juanell's surprise party.

When you observe, you report the facts. You don't interpret the facts. You don't jump to any conclusions about the facts. You don't give any special meaning to the facts. And you don't judge the facts. You only describe what you observe.

Observing sounds easy to do, but most people find it is difficult because of their habits. Because you are used to judging, changing the judging habit will take some effort.

LIFT YOUR SPIRITS

Before you go to sleep at night, take a few minutes and read something inspirational. You will feel good and fall asleep thinking positive thoughts instead of negative thoughts. The following, written by an anonymous source and quoted in <u>Success Is The Quality of Your Journey</u> by Jennifer James, is an example of something you could read before bed.

People are unreasonable, illogical, and self-centered.
Love them anyway.
If you do good, people may accuse you of selfish motives.
Do good anyway.
If you are successful, you may win false friends and true enemies.
Succeed anyway.
The good you do today may be forgotten tomorrow.
Do good anyway.
Honesty and transparency make you vulnerable.
Be honest and transparent anyway.
What you spend years building may be destroyed overnight.
Build anyway.
People who really want help may attack you if you help them.
Help anyway.
Give the world the best you have and you may get hurt.
Give the world your best anyway.
The world is full of conflict.
Choose peace of mind anyway.

You may be wondering how you can distinguish between two people if you do not compare them. There are two ways. First, use the word *preference*, which we talked about in earlier units. Preference avoids the comparison/judgment trap. Instead of saying, "She is so much smarter than her sister," you can say, "She prefers to read, and her sister prefers to draw." Neither person is put down. Each person is described without judgment.

Imagine that you work in an office. Perhaps people are waiting for their work to be typed, as in Illustration 6-3. Your boss could come in and say, "You're so slow. No one else gets behind like this." That's a comparison and a judgment that leads to feelings of low self-esteem. How could this situation be handled differently?

Instead of comparing you to someone else, the boss could evaluate your performance. When you **evaluate**, you compare something (in this case your behavior) to a standard. The focus is not on you as a person. You are not your behavior. You are not your thoughts or feelings, either. Your thoughts and feelings are part of you, but they are not the same as you.

Illustration 6-3

Meeting standards

When your behavior is evaluated, you are told specifically whether you are meeting the standards or not. The boss could say to you, "There are six people waiting on their work. Our goal is that no one waits. You need to key and proofread faster." This comment does not judge. It lets you know that something needs to be corrected and how to correct it.

Now let's imagine that you notice you are getting behind. You could say to yourself, "No one else gets behind like this." Whoops, comparison and judgment again. Instead of judging yourself, you could say, "I'm behind on my work. I need to work a little faster." You can evaluate your own performance. You could also talk to yourself using "prefer." You could say something like this, "I prefer not to get behind, so I'm going to work ahead of the projects that are coming in."

Observation and evaluation are so different from comparison and judgment! When you begin practicing these new skills, you will notice a big change in how you feel about yourself.

✔ CHECKPOINT 6-3

YOUR GOAL:
Get 6 or more
answers correct.

Read through each of the following comparisons. Change each to an observation. An example has been completed for you. Give yourself two points for each correct answer.

● I'm not sociable like my friends.

I prefer for someone else to start a conversation with

me. Then I feel comfortable and can talk easily.

1. My friend has such a nice car, and mine is such a clunker.

   _____

2. Everyone is married except me.

   _____

3. Lynn would have known what to do in this situation. I'm such a klutz.

   _____

4. No one is ever late to work except me.

   _____

5. Everybody reads better than I do.

   _____

6. My clothes aren't as nice as other people's.

   _____

7. I can't stand up for myself like Carlos can.

   _____

8. Why can't I lose weight on this diet like Frieda did?

   _____

☞ *Check your work. Record your score.*

YOU ARE UNIQUE

The sad thing about comparing is that you don't need to do it. The truth is, no one else in the whole world is like you. You are **unique**. You are one of a kind. Even your fingerprints are unique, as shown in Illustration 6-4. Comparing yourself to anyone else is unnecessary and pointless. No one can be you, and you can't be anyone else. When you try to be someone you're not, you suffer from low self-esteem.

Illustration 6-4

Fingerprints

Instead of wondering why you aren't more like someone else, you need to focus on what makes you unique. What qualities are special about you? What are your strengths? What kinds of experiences have you had that make you who you are today? What do you like to do? What do you do well? How would you describe yourself?

You may be thinking, "I'm not unique, there's nothing special about me." But you're wrong. Has a friend or family member of yours ever died? Can someone else replace her or him? No. Others might have similar qualities, or enjoy the same things, or do some of the same things. But no one is exactly like the person you lost. He or she was unique. And so are you! So is each person.

Try looking for what makes people different, or unique, when you meet them. Notice the difference, don't judge it. You'll feel better, and they will, too.

CHECKPOINT 6-4

YOUR GOAL:
Get 4 answers correct.

Read the following phrases. Decide if a phrase describes what makes you unique. If it does, write *yes* in the space provided. Write *no* if it does not. An example has been completed for you. Give yourself one point for each correct answer.

- <u> yes </u>   Fingerprints

1. _____   Your strengths

2. _____   What you like to do

3. _____   Your personal experiences

4. _____   What you enjoy

☞ *Check your work. Record your score.*

WHAT YOU HAVE LEARNED

Comparisons are one more way that you judge yourself. You can compare yourself with other people, or an ideal. Comparison damages your self-esteem. Instead of *comparing*, you want to *observe* differences. If you describe what you observe, you avoid judgment. If you want to develop yourself, you can evaluate your skills or behavior without judging yourself. Comparisons aren't needed because each person is unique.

ACTIVITY 6-1   **YOUR GOAL:** Get 5 or more answers correct.

Answer the following questions. Give yourself one point for each correct answer.
An example has been completed for you.

- Why do we compare ourselves with others?

  <u>Because we learned to compare ourselves with others as children.</u>

  <u>Comparing is a habit that lowers our self-esteem.</u>

1. Why does comparing lower our self-esteem?

   _____

2. If comparing can lower self-esteem, why do people keep doing it?

   _____

3. How is comparing related to prejudice?

   _____

4. How can you break the comparing habit?

   _____

5. Explain how if you come out ahead in a comparison you still might not
   feel good about yourself.

   _____

6. How can you tell someone he or she isn't doing something right if you
   can't compare?

   _____

☞ *Check your work. Record your score.*

ACTIVITY 6-2   **YOUR GOAL:** Earn 10 points.

Write a paragraph that describes how you are unique. For ideas about the kinds of things to include in your paragraph, reread the section in this unit titled YOU ARE UNIQUE. Give yourself ten points for your completed paragraph.

_____

_____

_____

_____

_____

_____

_____

_____

_____

_____

☞ *Check your work. Record your score.*

UNIT 7
PERFECTIONISM

WHAT YOU WILL LEARN

When you finish this unit, you will be able to:

- Identify the characteristics of a perfectionist.
- Identify the difference between perfectionism and self-awareness.

"Good, better, best. Never let it rest, until good is better and better is best."

"If you can't do it right, don't do it."

"A place for everything and everything in its place."

"If it's worth doing, it's worth doing right."

Did you hear any of these sayings as you were growing up? They all send the same message — Be Perfect. Being perfect is an example of a being should. All shoulds, and especially being shoulds, hurt your self-esteem. If you live with this should — if you try to do things "right" and be perfect — then you'll find this unit of particular interest.

WHAT IS A PERFECTIONIST?

A **perfectionist** is a person who believes there is one right or correct way to do things. There is a right way to fold clothes, a right way to wash the car, a right way to pay the bills, a right way to talk on the phone, and on and on. There is a right way to BE.

The Judge compares every action, every thought, every word against the standard of perfection. If two people do something differently, the Judge of the perfectionist quickly decides who is right and who is wrong. Instead of measuring success by what has been done, the Judge notices what hasn't been done.

LIFT YOUR SPIRITS

At the end of the day, you may think back over mistakes you made or things you said that you wished you hadn't. This review of what didn't go well can make you feel bad. Why not try something different for the next week? Each night before you go to bed, take five minutes to write down 10 things you did during the day that you feel good about. These don't need to be big things. They can be small things like, "I got up on time, I stopped when the light turned yellow, I smiled at a stranger, I hugged my child." You are noticing the things you did well instead of the things you did poorly. At the end of the week, you will have a list of 70 things you feel good about! Then the next time you feel down, you can read your list. You may like this so much you will want to keep adding to your list after the week is over.

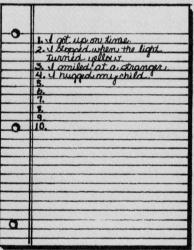

Perfectionism Causes Stress

Trying to be perfect creates stress. Why? Because human beings aren't perfect. Each person is *unique*. Unique does not mean perfect. You may do some tasks perfectly because that is the standard that is required. But doing a job perfectly is not the same as expecting to BE perfect. Perfectionists often confuse a job well done with being perfect. It is wiser to strive for excellence than to strive for perfection.

If you are trying to decide if a task needs to be done perfectly, ask yourself these questions:

1. What will it cost me in time or money to do it perfectly?
2. What are the likely consequences if I don't do it perfectly?

There is another reason being perfect is stressful. In any situation, a perfectionist needs to know or figure out what perfect is. This need makes decisions, in particular, hard to make. Sometimes you don't know what the "right" decision is. Instead of asking yourself what you want, you try to figure out the perfect solution. Sometimes there isn't a perfect solution. The perfectionist who keeps looking for the perfect solution will be unable to make any decision at all.

CHECKPOINT 7-1

YOUR GOAL:
Get 5 or more answers correct.

Read each of the following situations. Decide if a task needs to be done perfectly, or if it is okay to just get it done. Write the word *yes* if it requires perfection in the space provided. Write *no* if it does not. An example has been completed for you. Give yourself one point for each correct answer.

- ●   <u> no </u>   Washing the dishes.

1.   _____   Perform eye surgery.

2.   _____   Complete a homework assignment.

3.   _____   Picking fruits or vegetables.

4.   _____   Preparing a space shuttle for liftoff.

5.   _____   Dialing a phone number.

6.   _____   Painting a room.

☞ *Check your work. Record your score.*

The Benefits of Perfection

Why do people try to be perfect if it isn't possible? Because there are rare moments when everything comes together just right. There are moments when things appear to be perfect. And it feels so good! Everything seems to be right with the world. It's easy to think that if it could happen once, then it could happen again. If you created perfection one time, then if you try hard you can do it again. Like comparing, perfection becomes a vicious circle.

When you do manage to do something perfectly, there is often praise from others. They tell you what a great job you did. They tell you how proud they are of you. These compliments feel good. You want more of them. You think to yourself that if you can do it all perfectly again, you'll get more of these good feeling compliments.

For many people, that's how perfectionism started. As children they were praised when they did things right. If they made a mistake, a parent might have yelled at them or withdrawn love in some way. The child understood this to mean that he or she was only worthy when everything was perfect. The child didn't know that there is a difference between behavior and who you are.

Imagine that a child is at the table eating dinner and spills some milk. The parent might jump up and say, "Why can't you be more careful!?" as she or he cleans the mess. The child could easily interpret this to mean that she or he is not okay. After a series of similar situations, the child might decide being perfect is necessary to be loved. The child will not feel happy like the girl in Illustration 7-1, who is loved for who she is.

Illustration 7-1

Acceptance

It is easy to understand how a child would come to this conclusion. But why do adults continue trying to be perfect when they know it is impossible? The answer is simple: they believe it will give them self-worth. If they can just get it "right," they will feel okay about themselves. It seems logical that the closer you get to the ideal of perfection the higher your self-esteem. But that's not what happens.

The High Price Of Being Perfect

Each time you do something perfectly, there are other times when you don't measure up. Those times point out the truth -- you aren't perfect. And your self-esteem sinks. Even in those rare moments of perfection, there is still the awareness that you aren't perfect. There are times when you didn't do it right. Thus, the moments of feeling good are almost immediately followed by feelings of self-doubt and "Yes, but . . ."

In other words, you may have handled this situation well, but there was one last week that you didn't handle well. You're still not perfect, no matter how hard you try. You're still not okay.

LIFT YOUR SPIRITS

Perfection is not the key to success. A belief in yourself and persistence lead to success. Thomas Edison invented the light bulb — after 17,000 trials. Someone said to him, how could you go on after all those failures? Edison replied, "I never failed. I continued to discover more ways that would not work."

The perfectionist has trouble accepting a compliment. When someone says something positive, the perfectionist often answers "Yes, but . . ." For example, imagine a friend tells you that you did a great job fixing the car. If you're a perfectionist, you'll answer something like this, "Yes, but it took a lot longer than it should have." You don't accept the compliment or see what you did well. You can only see what is missing. You look for evidence that you aren't perfect, yet.

The core of the perfectionists' problem is that they don't feel worthy as human beings. So they cling to the mistaken belief that if they could be perfect, they would feel worthy. What a cruel game. It creates expectations the perfectionists can never meet. They don't see that they create their own suffering.

"I should be perfect." That is the irrational belief. You need to replace it with an affirming belief. Here are some examples:

I am unique, not perfect.

I will make mistakes and that is okay.

I do the best I can.

When you are trapped by a perfectionist belief system, you become rigid. You stop seeing choices. You see only one way—your way, the right way. You aren't as open as a person who isn't a perfectionist.

CHECKPOINT 7-2

YOUR GOAL:
Get 4 or more answers correct.

Some of the following expectations are realistic. Some of them are perfectionistic. Write the letter *R* in the space provided if you think an expectation is realistic. Write the letter *P* if you think the expectation is perfectionistic. An example has been completed for you. Give yourself one point for each correct answer.

●   __P__   I expect to fix the broken screen door the first time I try.

1.   _____   I expect to listen to my children any time they want to talk to me.

2.   _____   I expect to pass the test without studying.

3.   _____   I expect that I'll need to practice before I get good at baseball.

4.   _____   I expect that I will be disappointed from time to time.

5. _____   I expect to understand this the first time I read it.

☞ *Check your work. Record your score.*

You thought being perfect would bring acceptance and love from other people. But just the opposite occurs. Your rigidity turns people away. It is not easy to be around a person who does everything according to a rule book.

Your judgment turns people away. They know that if you judge yourself this harshly, you will surely judge them. People don't like to be judged. It lowers their self-esteem. It might be helpful to ask yourself the question Jerry Jampolsky, author and psychiatrist, asks: "Would you rather be right, or would you rather be happy?"

Your unrealistic standards turn others away. They know before they do anything that you will be running right behind them fixing or correcting what they did. Or you might tell them how to fix or change what they did. Life is hard enough without this added stress.

Your seriousness turns others away. Perfection is serious business. It requires a great deal of control. If the perfectionist lets go of the reins and lets things just happen, something might not be done right. Most adults don't like someone trying to control them.

You may be thinking, I'm not like that! Perhaps not. But if you've ever thought of yourself as a perfectionist, or if you've been told that you are, this may be how others react to you. The only way to know for sure is to ask people you trust.

The F Word — Failure

Unfortunately, when people make a mistake they often think it makes them a failure as a person. To think making a mistake is the same as being a failure is an irrational belief. People aren't failures. You are not the same as what you do.

A mistake is just that — a mistake. Something did not turn out the way you would have preferred. You have four choices when you make a mistake.

1. Take action to correct the mistake.
2. Apologize and accept the consequences of the mistake.

LIFT YOUR SPIRITS

People who are perfectionists tend to look for what others do wrong. They tend to criticize. You will feel better about yourself if you try to catch people doing things right. Then tell them about it! This will also make other people want to be around you. Make a goal to give out three compliments every day.

3. Learn from the mistake so you don't repeat it in the future.

4. Judge yourself and feel bad.

You will notice that the fourth choice does not fix the mistake, or prevent it in the future. The fourth choice wastes time and energy. You cannot go back in time and undo what you've done. If you sit and watch reruns of your mistake and judge yourself a failure because of it, you're wasting your life.

Expressions like:

"If only. . ."

"Why didn't I?"

"I should have. . ."

tell you that you're judging your mistakes instead of accepting them. It's not the mistake that hurts your self-esteem, it's what you say to yourself about the mistake.

You grow through mistakes. That's how children learn to crawl, walk, talk, and do all the other skills. First they fail. First they make mistakes. They know:

If it's worth doing well, it's worth doing poorly.

In other words, if something is worth learning, we won't be good at it at first. It will take some time to practice. We will make some mistakes as we go. That's a normal part of learning. Instead of criticizing mistakes, look for the progress that is being made.

If you aren't making mistakes, it isn't a sign that you're a perfect person. It is more likely a sign that you aren't trying anything new. You aren't growing. You aren't taking any risks. Success comes when you are willing to make mistakes and learn from them. Maturity comes when you are willing to accept the consequences of your mistakes and keep on trying.

✔ CHECKPOINT 7-3

YOUR GOAL:
Get 4 or more answers correct.

Listed below are examples of mistakes people have made. Write what you think would be the best way to handle each situation in the space provided. An example has been completed for you. Give yourself one point for each correct answer.

● You waited until the last minute to start your homework, and you didn't finish it before class started.

Next time start your homework earlier.

1. You got into a fight with Hiro and said things you didn't mean. Now Hiro doesn't want to talk to you.

_____

2. When you were mowing the yard, you cut down some flowers the kids had planted.

  _____

3. You're late to work.

  _____

4. You borrowed a sweater from Marilyn and spilled something on it.

  _____

5. You miss all the questions on a Checkpoint.

  _____

☞ *Check your work. Record your score.*

LET GO OF YOUR PERFECTIONISM

Can you picture yourself sitting and reading this book while you are reading it? Can you notice how you are feeling? Can you notice what you are thinking? This ability to act and at the same time observe yourself acting is called **self-awareness**. Only human beings can do this. Animals cannot.

Self-awareness is very helpful if you are going to let go of your perfectionism. You are not simply your actions. Many people think that what they do is who they are. But if you are your actions, then who is observing you? If you do something wrong, it doesn't make *you* wrong.

Sometimes you think you are what you feel. But have you ever noticed yourself being angry? Maybe you wanted to stop saying unkind things and yet you watched yourself say them anyway. Perhaps you have observed yourself singing when you were happy. Maybe you have observed yourself feeling excited about going somewhere or seeing someone. If you are your feelings, would you be able to observe yourself feeling those feelings? Even if you don't like the way you feel, that doesn't make *you* unlikable.

Have you ever observed yourself thinking about something? Maybe you were trying to solve a problem. Maybe you sat at the table and thought about which bills to pay first. If you were your thoughts, you wouldn't be able to observe yourself thinking.

Who you are is much more than your thoughts, feelings, or actions. Those are all ways that you express your real self in the world. But you are more than that. The real you is that awareness, or observing self.

When you were a child, your actions were often confused with the real you. For example, if you didn't want to share with

LIFT YOUR SPIRITS

"to be nobody but yourself

in a world which is doing

its best day and night to

make you everybody else

means to fight the hardest

battle which any

human being can

fight and never

stop fighting."

e.e. cummings

another child, you might have been told you were a "bad girl/boy." If you heard this over and over, you might have started to believe you were bad, or not okay. But remember, you are more than your behavior. You may not have shared, but that is not the same as being bad.

Perhaps when you were a child something happened that scared you and you cried. An adult may have said, "You shouldn't feel that way. Stop your crying." If you were told over and over that how you felt wasn't okay, you may have come to feel that there was something wrong with you. But you are more than your feelings.

Most of the time you are so busy living your life that you don't observe yourself. You are unaware. If you can remember that you are more than your thoughts, feelings, or behavior, you can like yourself even when you aren't perfect.

CHECKPOINT 7-4

YOUR GOAL:
Get 4 answers correct.

Write the word that will complete the following statements in the space provided. Choose your answer from the list of words provided. An example has been completed for you. Give yourself one point for each correct answer.

like   observe   real self
self-awareness   let go

● Self-awareness will help you <u>let go</u> of your perfectionism.

1.   The ability to act, and at the same time observe yourself acting, is called _____.

2. When you _____ how you think, feel or act, you avoid judgment.

3. Sometimes our actions are confused with our

    _____.

4. Self-awareness helps you _____ yourself, even when you aren't perfect.

☞ *Check your work. Record your score.*

WHAT YOU HAVE LEARNED

When you want to do things right, when you want to BE perfect, you are a perfectionist. Perfectionism is an attempt to escape feelings of worthlessness. You believe that if you are perfect, you'll be okay. But trying to be perfect causes lots of stress and can cause other people to withdraw from you. You can let go of perfectionism if you give yourself permission to make mistakes. You can let go if you accept that you are more than your thoughts, feelings, and behaviors.

ACTIVITY 7-1 **YOUR GOAL:** Get 8 or more answers correct.

Read each of the following statements. If a statement is true, put a *T* in the space provided. If it is false, put an *F* in the space provided. An example has been completed for you. Give yourself one point for each correct answer.

-   __F__   Perfectionism is something you inherit.

1. _____ People who are perfectionists want to do everything right.

2. _____ Perfectionists are loved by everyone.

3. _____ One way to build your self-esteem is to become a perfectionist.

4. _____ Perfectionists feel bad when they make a mistake.

5. _____ Making a mistake is the same thing as being a failure.

6. _____ Rigidity, seriousness, and unrealistic expectations are qualities of a perfectionist.

7. _____ Perfectionists feel lots of stress.

8. _____ If you accept your mistakes, you can raise your self-esteem.

9. _____ Perfectionism is a form of judgment.

10. _____ Only perfectionists do a good job.

☞ *Check your work. Record your score.*

ACTIVITY 7-2 YOUR GOAL: Get 4 or more answers correct.

Answer each of the following questions in the space provided. An example has been completed for you. Give yourself one point for each correct answer.

- Where does perfectionism come from?

  Most people learn it in childhood. They think that they are
  _____

  expected to be perfect to be okay. They keep believing this when
  _____

  they grow up.
  _____

1. What are the four choices you have when you make a mistake?

   _____

   _____

2. What is self-awareness?

   _____

   _____

3. List three disadvantages of being a perfectionist.

   _____

   _____

   _____

4. What would you need to do if you wanted to stop being a perfectionist?

   _____

   _____

5. Explain how perfectionism can cause stress.

   _____

   _____

☞ *Check your work. Record your score.*

PART THREE
BUILD YOUR SELF-ESTEEM

UNIT 8
KNOW THYSELF

UNIT 9
EXPRESS YOURSELF

UNIT 10
KNOW YOUR VALUES

UNIT 11
POSITIVE SELF-TALK

UNIT 12
I LIKE MYSELF!

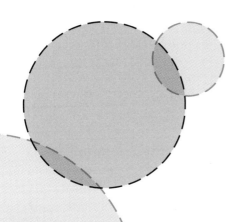

UNIT 8
KNOW THYSELF

WHAT YOU WILL LEARN

When you finish this unit, you will be able to:

- Describe your talents.
- Describe your skills.
- Identify areas to develop.

Did you know that you are President of a company called YOU, Inc.? As President, you make decisions about where you work, who your friends are, where you live, and how you spend your money. You may not realize it, but you market and sell yourself everyday. The better you know yourself, the better you will be able to represent yourself.

People who have low self-esteem have trouble telling you who they are. When an employer asks a person with low self-esteem to tell a little bit about him or herself, there is a long pause. What can they say?

When you meet someone new who says, "Tell me about yourself," do you know what to say? What do you say when a potential landlord wants to know a little bit about you?

You are put on the spot several times every week to promote YOU, Inc. What kind of job are you doing? In this unit, you'll learn more about yourself. In fact, you'll be able to write a 60-second "commercial" about YOU.

You want to know your talents and skills so well that you can describe yourself in 60 seconds or less. The next time you interview for a job and are asked about yourself, you will know what to say! If an instructor at school asks you to introduce yourself, you'll know what to say.

WHAT ARE YOUR TALENTS?

Every person is born with certain talents or gifts. A **talent** is a natural ability; it is something that you can do easily. Because talents seem to come "naturally," you may not even know what talents you have. You may think that everyone can do what you do with the same ease. Not true. Because a talent feels easy to you, you may not take it seriously.

Your talents are part of what makes you unique. A talent is not something that you learn. Either you have it or you don't. People often believe they don't have any talents. They see talents in other people but not in themselves.

For example, some people know how to put colors together in a pleasing way. They might use this talent in how they dress or decorate their homes. Their eye for color is a gift. Other people know how to fix things. They can take just about anything apart and put it together again. An eye for color and fixing things are different talents. One talent is not better than another. Talents are different and equally important.

You can use these cues to identify when someone has a gift or talent:

They make it look easy, effortless;

They do it with grace or beauty;

They appear to have a knack;

They appear to enjoy it.

Jesse Jackson, in Illustration 8-1, shows his gift for public speaking.

Illustration 8-1

Jesse Jackson
Gifted Speaker

► LIFT YOUR SPIRITS

One way to discover your talents is to think about things you enjoy. Think of three times when you have done something that you felt good about. Write a few sentences about each of these times. Then ask yourself, "What do these three situations have in common?" The answer can be a clue to your talents. Most people enjoy doing things that come easily to them.

Another reason people think they don't have talents is because they think only famous people have talents. In other words, you need to be a famous movie star, rock star, or sports figure to have talent. Not true. Each person expresses his or her talent in a unique way. Because one person gains fame does not mean he or she is talented and that someone without fame is untalented. That is a comparison. Remember, comparisons can lower self-esteem.

The last reason that you sometimes don't realize your talents is that they may not be valued in our society. For example, a talent for tracking animals would have been valued in the 1800s when people hunted for their food. Today most people buy their food in a store. To find your talents, you need to look for what you enjoy and what you are good at, not just what society says is a talent.

There are many different types of talents. Some examples include:

music	organizing
athletic ability	numbers
taste	listening
artistic ability	eye/hand coordination
leadership	mechanical
language	sense of humor
public speaking	relating to animals

The list goes on and on. The important question is, "What are your talents?"

CHECKPOINT 8-1

YOUR GOAL:
Get 6 or more points.

List three of your talents. In a sentence or two, tell why you think each is a talent. An example has been completed for you. Give yourself three points for each talent you list and explain.

● I have a talent for remembering things. I can meet someone one time and remember the name and face. I don't need to make a list when I go to the store because I can remember what to get. I can even remember phone numbers.

1. _____

   _____

2. _____

   _____

3. _____

   _____

☞ *Check your work. Record your score.*

WHAT ARE YOUR SKILLS?

A **skill** is a developed ability that requires the use of the hands, body, or mind. It is something you have learned to do. You may have learned it from a teacher, by watching someone else do it, or through trial and error. Usually, practice is necessary to get good at a skill. Unlike a talent, it does not come naturally. Your talents can make it easier or harder to learn a skill, however.

For example, if you have athletic ability — talent — it will be easier for you to learn how to play basketball than for the person who has a musical gift. If you have a gift of eye/hand coordination, it will be easier for you to learn keyboarding than for a person who has artistic abilities.

More Skills, More Choices

Most people have dozens of skills. The more skills you have, the more you will feel in control of your life. Here's why.

Imagine that you are a painter. That is the only job skill you have. What will happen if people don't want painters anymore? What if people want to wallpaper their homes instead of paint them? If painting is your only skill, you are out of work.

But if you paint *and* wallpaper, there will still be work for you. By having more than one skill, you are more in control of your future. Imagine that you also know how to hang dry wall. Now you have even more choices. As President of YOU, Inc., the more skills you have, the more secure your company.

As times change, different skills are needed. The person who has only one skill may find him or herself out of work. The person who has several skills will be able to adapt to changes in the workplace. For example, ten years ago very few secretaries used computers. Today, without computer skills a secretary like the one in Illustration 8-2 probably wouldn't find a job. Are you keeping your skills up-to-date?

Illustration 8-2

Secretaries Have
Many Skills

Think of an accomplishment or achievement from your past. What did you do? How did you feel about it? What skills did you use? Can you think of other times when you have used those same skills?

Add Skills and Add Value

As you add skills, you become more valuable to others. You are **versatile**. You are versatile when you are capable of doing many things. People want to hire someone who is versatile. You are in more demand. That gives you more choices and more control. You'll feel more self-confident and in charge of your life.

Versatility applies at home, too. The more skills you have, the more control you feel. If you have a broken step and you know how to use a hammer and saw, you can fix the step. If you lose a button and you know how to sew one on, you can fix your shirt or blouse. If your faucet drips and you know how to change a washer, you can stop the drip. If your child starts to choke and you know the Heimlich maneuver, you could save his or her life.

When you feel in control of your life, there is less stress. The more versatile you are, the more likely it is that you will have high self-esteem. Building skills makes sense!

Do you know what your skills are? Knowing your skills is an important part of writing your 60-second commercial. You need to know what you can do. Are you versatile? To help you make your list of skills, Checkpoint 8-2 gives you some common categories.

✔ ## CHECKPOINT 8-2

YOUR GOAL:
Get 10 points.

List your skills. The following categories will help you get started. Put an X in the space provided beside any skill you believe you have. Write in skills you have that are not listed in the spaces provided. Give yourself ten points for completing this Checkpoint.

AT HOME

_____ cooking
_____ cleaning
_____ budgeting
_____ shopping
_____ repairing
_____ gardening
_____
_____
_____

ON THE JOB

_____ telephone skills
_____ using special equipment
_____ keyboarding
_____ filing
_____ sorting
_____ operating machinery
_____
_____
_____

PERSONAL		WITH PEOPLE	
_____	grooming	_____	parenting
_____	driving	_____	supervising
_____	sewing	_____	communicating
_____	dancing	_____	problem solving
_____	playing games or sports	_____	decision making

_____ _____

_____ _____

_____ _____

OTHER SKILLS

_____

_____

_____

_____

☞ *Check your work. Record your score.*

DEVELOPING TALENTS AND SKILLS

You may be feeling confused about the difference between a talent and a skill. They work together in ways that can be confusing.

Develop Your Talents With Skills

Think of a talent as being like a diamond in the rough. For a diamond to be most valuable, it needs to be cut and polished. Some diamonds are cut better than others. The better a diamond is cut, the more beautiful and valuable it becomes.

If your talents are like the diamond, then the skills you develop are like the cutting and polishing. The more skills you develop around your talents, the more powerful your talent becomes. The more practiced you become at your skills, the better you can make your talent shine. Great musicians, great athletes — anyone who is outstanding in his or her field — practice everyday the skills that make the talent shine.

If you don't develop some skills around your talents, it is like leaving a diamond in the rough. The talent isn't worth as much. When you develop your talents with skills, the result is greater than the talent or the skills alone.

> ## LIFT YOUR SPIRITS
>
> The Bible tells the story of three servants who were each given money (called *talents*) by their master to manage while he was gone. The first servant was given five talents which he doubled. The second servant was given two talents which he doubled. The master rewarded both servants when he returned. The third servant was given one talent, which he buried. When the master returned, this servant gave back the one talent. The master was upset that the servant buried the talent and did not use it.

Are you building skills around your talents? If you are, then you are making the most of your gifts. You're making more out of them than they are alone.

Develop Skills When You Don't Have Talent

What if you don't have a particular talent? Perhaps you weren't born with a natural ability for organization. When things are a mess, you don't know where to start to put them back in order. If you want to be organized, what do you do? You develop skills that will help you be organized, even though you don't have a talent for organization.

If you don't have a gift for taste, you can follow a recipe when you cook. You can develop cooking skills. If you don't have mechanical talent, you can learn about how mechanical things work and follow instructions. If you don't have musical talent, you can work with a voice coach to learn how to sing.

Here's a surprising fact. People who develop skills and practice them regularly can often perform as well as a person with a gift that is undeveloped.

Are you using your talents? Are you limiting yourself by saying you can't do something because you aren't talented?

CHECKPOINT 8-3

YOUR GOAL:
Get 4 or more answers correct.

Write the word that will complete the following statements in the space provided. Choose your answer from the list of words provided. An example has been completed for you. Give yourself one point for each correct answer.

powerful   skills   talent

• A <u>talent</u> is like a diamond in the rough.

1. _____ are like cutting and polishing a diamond.

2. The more skills you develop around a talent, the more _____ it becomes.

3. If you don't have a particular talent, you can develop

    _____.

4. When you develop skills, you can perform as well as a
    person with undeveloped _____.

5. People who are outstanding in their fields have both
    _____ and _____.

☞ *Check your work. Record your score.*

DEVELOP YOURSELF!

In the past, you could stop learning when you left high school.
The skills you learned there would last a lifetime. Most people
worked the same job all of their adult lives. Today, you need to
be a lifelong learner. If you are like the average person, you will
make at least seven job changes and have several careers.

As your job changes, or as you change jobs, there will be new
things for you to learn. New skills to develop. New ways to use
your talents. As you get to know yourself better, you will become
aware of undeveloped areas. Bosses, friends, co-workers, and
family members will point out areas in which you can grow.

With so many areas for personal development, you can feel
overwhelmed at times. You might be tempted to criticize yourself
because you aren't perfect. Don't judge yourself when you
become aware of an undeveloped area. Accept yourself. Then
decide what approach you will use to respond to the undeveloped
area.

Take No Action

Sometimes you will become aware of an undeveloped area that
isn't important to you. You will decide to leave it undeveloped.
You don't need to apologize for your choice or feel bad. Here are
some examples.

Playing tennis is an undeveloped area for Annette. She just
can't seem to get the hang of it. She doesn't really enjoy playing,
either. She decides to leave it an undeveloped area.

George doesn't know how to repair his car when it breaks
down. He's never been interested in getting under the hood of a
car. He decides to leave this an undeveloped area and hire a
mechanic when he has car problems.

Postpone Action

Sometimes you will want to learn more than you can at one time.
Then you need to decide what to do first. You don't have to do it

all to be okay! Some undeveloped areas may need to wait. Here are some examples.

Raoul decided not to join the community choir because he can't sing on key. That's an undeveloped area that he may decide to work on someday. First, he's going to concentrate on his studies.

Maureen had planned to learn more about gardening this year. After her job change, she decided to learn new job skills instead. She plans to come back to gardening when she is more comfortable in her job.

Take Action

As President of YOU, Inc., there are some undeveloped areas that you will decide to act on now. These will be areas that are important to you. Sometimes you will see the undeveloped area yourself. Other times an important person like a spouse, friend, or boss will tell you about the undeveloped area. Here are some examples:

Timothy isn't a very good cook. Cooking is an undeveloped area he decided to work on. Now he's taking a cooking class at the community college.

Jan isn't a good file sorter yet. Her boss wants her to develop this skill, and she wants to improve, too. She is practicing and knows she will get better.

✔ CHECKPOINT 8-4

YOUR GOAL:
Get 3 or more answers correct.

Read the following situations. Decide how you would respond to each undeveloped area and why. Would you take action, postpone action, or take no action? Write your answer, telling what you would do and why you would do it, in the space provided. An example has been completed for you. Give yourself two points for each correct answer.

● Kim has two pre-school children. She is going to school part-time in addition to working. Kim has always wanted to learn how to bowl. She has been invited to join a beginners league. What would you do?

Postpone action. Kim has enough to do right now. She

can learn to bowl when she's out of school or when the

kids are older.

1. Lynn doesn't know how to drive. She's been meaning to learn for years. Her mother is ill now and can't drive.

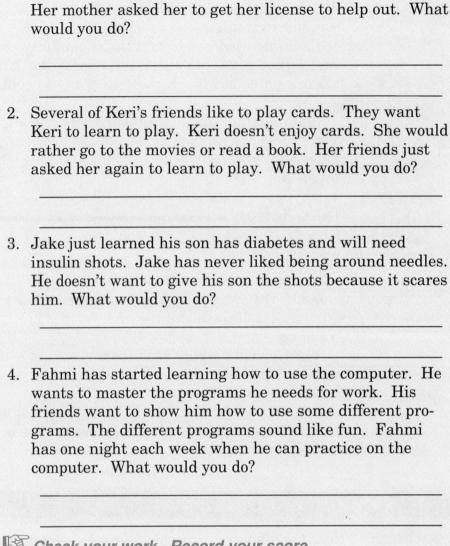

Her mother asked her to get her license to help out. What would you do?

_____

_____

2. Several of Keri's friends like to play cards. They want Keri to learn to play. Keri doesn't enjoy cards. She would rather go to the movies or read a book. Her friends just asked her again to learn to play. What would you do?

_____

_____

3. Jake just learned his son has diabetes and will need insulin shots. Jake has never liked being around needles. He doesn't want to give his son the shots because it scares him. What would you do?

_____

_____

4. Fahmi has started learning how to use the computer. He wants to master the programs he needs for work. His friends want to show him how to use some different programs. The different programs sound like fun. Fahmi has one night each week when he can practice on the computer. What would you do?

_____

_____

☞ *Check your work. Record your score.*

Having undeveloped areas does not make you bad. That is a judgment that lowers your self-esteem. Having undeveloped areas is part of what makes you human. Use your undeveloped areas to be a lifelong learner with high self-esteem.

WHAT YOU HAVE LEARNED

Each person has talents, skills, and undeveloped areas. You need to know what your talents are so that you can build skills around them. The more skills you have, the more versatile you are. You can develop skills in areas where you lack talent. You need to know your undeveloped areas so that you can develop them or accept them.

ACTIVITY 8-1   YOUR GOAL: Get 10 points.

Write a 60-second commercial for yourself. Use all the things you have learned about your talents, skills, and undeveloped areas. Describe who you are and what you can do. An example has been completed for you. Give yourself ten points for your commercial.

● I have a gift for taking things apart and putting them back together. I use this gift to fix things that break at home and to work on cars. I have taken courses to learn more about how to work on certain types of cars. I enjoy this work, and people like me to do it.

_____

_____

_____

_____

_____

☞ *Check your work. Record your score.*

ACTIVITY 8-2   YOUR GOAL: Get 6 or more answers correct.

Read each of the following statements. If a statement is true, put a *T* in the space provided. If it is false, put an *F* in the space provided. An example has been completed for you. Give yourself one point for each correct answer.

● ___T___ Talents and gifts are different words for the same thing.

1. _____ Some talents are better than other talents.

2. _____ Many people don't know what their talents are.

3. _____ Some people don't have any talents, which is why they have low self-esteem.

4. _____ Some people develop skills in areas where they don't have talents.

5. _____   All people have undeveloped areas.

6. _____   If you have talent, you don't need skills.

7. _____   Two people could do the same thing, and one could use talent while the other used skills.

8. _____   If you aren't famous, then you don't have talent.

☞ *Check your work. Record your score.*

UNIT 9
EXPRESS YOURSELF

WHAT YOU WILL LEARN

When you finish this unit, you will be able to:

- Choose how to express your feelings.
- Identify the four steps to expressing anger.
- Identify the causes of fear and how to overcome them.

It is important to know how you feel. If you try to deny a feeling — pretend that it isn't there — you will find that, over time, all feelings are denied. When you try to shut off feelings that hurt, you also shut off feelings that bring joy. You feel numb when you shut off your feelings. People with high self-esteem feel the whole range of human emotions from glad to sad, mad to scared.

Feelings are not "right" or "wrong." You feel what you feel. Don't say to someone, "You shouldn't feel like that." Different people can have different feelings in the same situation. What is important is to learn how to express feelings in a way that does not lower your self-esteem or someone else's.

CHOOSE HOW YOU EXPRESS YOUR FEELINGS

Some feelings feel good. Other feelings don't feel as good. Be careful that you don't judge yourself when your feelings aren't pleasant. If how you *feel* isn't okay, then who you are probably isn't okay, either. You want to accept how you feel. Then you can decide how you will act on the feeling.

For example, there may be a day when you don't feel like going to work. The feeling is okay. What's important is how you choose to act on the feeling. You don't need to be controlled by your feelings. They are only one ingredient that goes into who you are. Other ingredients are how you act, your goals, and your beliefs. The person with high self-esteem puts all of these parts together to make wise choices that will build his or her self-

LIFT YOUR SPIRITS

It is so easy to take other people for granted. And it is easy to think that other people know how we feel about them. Especially people we love. The truth is, most people are hungry to know how others feel about them. How long has it been since you said "I love you" to your parents? your brothers or sisters? your spouse? your children? your friends? Today tell three people that you love them.

esteem. You can go to work whether or not you "feel" like it. Successful people often do things they don't "feel" like doing. How often have you done something positive for yourself, even when you didn't feel like it? For example, study for a test instead of watching TV, or read a textbook instead of meeting with friends.

Just because you feel something does not mean you need to act on it. If you feel mad, you don't need to hit someone. If you feel hurt, you don't need to lash out at someone. Children show their feelings when they feel them. As an adult, you can make choices about when, where, and how you express your feelings. Choosing when, where, and how to express your feelings is part of growing up.

Admit Your Feeling

The first thing you need to do when you feel something is admit to yourself what you are feeling. You don't have to say how you feel to anyone else. It is enough for you to know. Don't hide your feelings from yourself! If you do, you can become physically or emotionally ill.

Next, decide how you want to express the feeling. Sometimes you will want to tell another person how you feel. Other times you will want to express the feeling without talking to another person.

One way to express a feeling without talking to someone is to put it in writing. You can write a letter that you don't send, or you can write in a diary. Some people do something physical to express their feelings, like playing a game of basketball or working in the garden. Other people use music to release their feelings. The important point is to express your feelings in a way that you won't regret later.

Hurting yourself or another person, yelling, destroying property, drinking, or the silent treatment are examples of ways people express feelings that don't work. These methods can lower your self-esteem. They can also have serious consequences, such as trouble with the law. Before you act on a feeling, think about the likely outcomes of your action.

CHECKPOINT 9-1

YOUR GOAL:
Get 6 or more points.

Read each situation and decide the best way to express the feeling. Place the letter of the correct answer in the space provided. An example has been completed for you. Give yourself two points for each correct answer.

- **b** Marion feels angry with her son.
  a. Hit the child
  b. Tell her son to go to his room while she calms down and decides what to do
  c. Leave home

1. _____ Sam wakes up tired and doesn't feel like going to work.
   a. Get up and go to work
   b. Call in sick
   c. Yell at the kids

2. _____ Sunita feels worried about a past-due electric bill.
   a. Swear at the people at the electric company
   b. Blame her husband for not making enough money
   c. Discuss her feelings with her husband and make a plan for how to pay the bill

3. _____ Joma feels hurt that his friend borrowed $20 and hasn't repaid it.
   a. Pick a fight
   b. Ask for the money
   c. Have a drink

4. _____ Linda took a new job and feels scared that she will make a mistake.
   a. Tell a friend how she is feeling
   b. Act like a know-it-all
   c. When the boss isn't around, pick on other people

☞ *Check your work. Record your score.*

The Danger of Mislabeling Your Feelings

Sometimes people use the wrong words to describe what they feel. This is called **mislabeling**. When you mislabel feelings, you often upset yourself. Let's look at an example.

Imagine that your instructor asks you a question, and you don't know the answer. Later you might say to yourself, "I feel stupid." Stupid isn't a feeling. Stupid is a judgment of yourself that makes you feel bad. It lowers your self-esteem.

In the same situation, you could describe your feelings with a feeling word. A word that isn't judgmental. You could say, "I felt embarassed when I didn't know the answer." Now you haven't damaged your self-esteem. You kept the Judge from talking to you. And you were honest with yourself about how you felt.

When you say "I feel . . . ," pay attention to the words you use next. Do you use feeling words like the ones in Illustration 9-1? Or are you using judgmental labels that lower your self-esteem?

Illustration 9-1

Feeling Words

Do you know the meaning of these words? Do you use them to describe how you feel? Add your own words to the list.

affectionate	awed	concerned	determined
free	grateful	generous	happy
lively	love	lonely	mad
moody	numb	peaceful	proud
passionate	pity	afraid	alone
thankful	abandoned	isolated	challenged
defiant	encouraged	sensitive	defeated
jealous	tender	lazy	strong
inadequate	pessimistic	discouraged	puzzled
thrilled	excited	shook	weary
suspicious	trust	vibrant	sad

EXPRESSING ANGER

There are some feelings that are harder than others to express. One of those feelings is anger. Many people don't know what to do when they feel angry. Rather than express it, they stuff it inside. If angry feelings are kept inside you, they can turn into something else. Sometimes anger held inside turns into depression. You start to feel down, and you lose your energy. For other people, anger vents itself on the body. The heart especially suffers when angry feelings are kept inside. Research proves that people who feel angry most of the time are more likely to have a heart attack than people who don't feel angry as often.

The point is, if you don't express your anger, you will find that it can make you sick — either physically or emotionally.

Is there a healthy way to express anger that won't lower your self-esteem? Yes. Follow these four steps the next time you feel mad, angry or upset.

Step 1: State how you feel beginning with the words "I feel. . ." It is important that you use the words, "I feel." With these words you own the feeling you have. Some people, when they feel angry, start with the words, "You make me. . ." If you start out with the word "you," your message will be blaming. It is as if you are pointing your finger at the other person. Blaming causes **defensiveness**. Defensiveness is trying to protect yourself from someone else's words. You can't solve a problem with blame or defensiveness.

Step 2: Describe what happened.
Keep your description as brief and simple as possible. The more you say, the greater the chance that there will be a misunderstanding between you and the other person. You want to present facts. You aren't adding your opinion or making any judgments. You aren't blaming. Here are some examples of Steps 1 and 2.
   "I feel angry when you come home late."
   "I feel mad when you leave your clothes on the floor."

   "I feel angry when the bus is late."
   Notice how different the preceding statements are from the following blaming, judgmental statements:
   "You are so inconsiderate!" (said in an angry tone when someone is late)
   "You make me mad when you act like a slob." (said to a child who didn't hang his or her clothes)
   "I hate the bus company!" (said when the bus is late)
   Which way do you talk to yourself and others?

✔ CHECKPOINT 9-2

YOUR GOAL:
Get 4 or more answers correct.

Read each of the following statements. If a statement is true, put a *T* in the space provided. If it is false, put an *F* in the space provided. An example has been completed for you.

● ___T___   Anger is a feeling that many people find hard to express.

1. _____   Keeping anger inside of you can make you sick.

2. _____   Anger makes your heart strong.

3. _____   The first step when you feel angry is to find someone to blame.

4. _____   When you say "You make me feel. . . ," you are blaming.

5. _____   The second step when expressing anger is to describe what happened.

☞ *Check your work. Record your score.*

LIFT YOUR SPIRITS

If you want to feel good, do something nice for another person and don't tell anyone about it. The joy will come from your action, not from praise for your action. You will be giving without expecting to get something back. The surprise is that you will get something back — a boost to your self-esteem.

Step 3: Ask yourself why you're upset.

Anger is a secondary feeling. That means it isn't the first feeling you feel. It comes second. You need to ask yourself what you felt first. Most of the time anger comes after a feeling of fear or hurt.

Have you ever expected someone to come home at a certain time, and he or she didn't? As you waited you may have started to feel scared and worried. You wondered if there was an accident, or if something else happened. When the person you were waiting for finally walked in the door and you saw that he or she was okay, you probably reacted with anger. The anger came after the fear.

Perhaps you have tried to keep a tidy house. You asked your family to help you by picking up their clothes instead of leaving them on the floor. When you come home from work and see clothes lying on the floor, your first feeling is probably one of hurt that your family did not honor your request. You are trying to keep the house nice, and no one is helping you. Rather than express your hurt, you probably react with feelings of anger.

The situation when the bus is late is another example when the first feeling is fear. If the bus is late, you might be afraid that you will get to work late.

When you add the third step to your first two steps, it sounds like this.

"I feel angry when you're late because I feel scared that something has happened to you."

"I feel mad when you leave your clothes on the floor because I feel hurt that you aren't keeping the house tidy."

"I feel angry when the bus is late because I feel afraid that I'll be late to work."

Step 4: Ask for what you want.

When you feel angry, you usually know what you want changed. The problem is that other people may not know what you want. If you think they can read your mind, you will be disappointed. You need to tell other people what you want different. You need to tell them if you want them to change how they act. If you skip this last step, you may feel frustrated that you expressed your anger and nothing happened.

After you express your feelings in Steps 1, 2, and 3, follow up with a request for action. Here are some examples:

"I feel angry when you're late because I feel scared that something has happened to you. If you are going to be late in the future, please call me."

"I feel mad when you leave your clothes on the floor because I feel hurt that you aren't keeping the house tidy. Please put your clothes away after you take them off."

"I feel angry when the bus is late because I feel afraid that I'll be late to work. Who can I talk to about this problem?"

The first few times that you try to follow these steps, they will seem strange. That's because they are new. After you practice them, you will find that you are able to express your anger without hurting your self-esteem or the self-esteem of others.

CHECKPOINT 9-3

YOUR GOAL:
Get 10 or more points.

Read each of the following situations. Write out how the person could express his or her anger in the space provided. Include each of the four steps in your answer. An example has been completed for you. Give yourself one point for each step that you include in your answer.

- Tom went to get his hammer, and it wasn't where he keeps it. One of the kids used it and didn't put it back. Tom was mad. And he was hurt that the kids didn't respect his things. Tom doesn't like spending time looking for things.

  <u>I feel mad when my tools aren't put back after you use</u>

  <u>them because it seems like you don't care about my things.</u>

  <u>That hurts. If you're going to use my tools, put them away</u>

  <u>when you're finished.</u>

1. Tricia was angry when her friend called at the last minute to cancel their plans. She felt hurt. She wondered how important she was to her friend. She thought her friend could have called sooner, so Tricia could have made other plans for herself.

  _____

  _____

  _____

2. Jose was mad when he got back his test paper. He got a "D". He was afraid he might not pass the class. He wished he could study more and take the test again.

_____

_____

_____

3. Helen was angry when her boyfriend told her he was taking a job to work night shift. She was afraid they wouldn't see each other anymore because she worked days. She couldn't understand why he didn't talk over his decision with her before he took the job.

_____

_____

_____

☞ *Check your work. Record your score.*

UNDERSTANDING FEAR

Another feeling that is hard to deal with is fear. Fear can stop you from doing things that could make you feel better about yourself. People react to fear in many ways. How do you usually cope with fear? Do you try to overcome it? deny it? avoid it? talk about it? ignore it?

Five Types of Fears

People feel afraid for many reasons. Which one(s) of these reasons fits you? Put a check mark on the line if you have felt this type of fear.

_____   **Fear of failure**

This is a fear that you won't be able to do something. You may worry that others will laugh at you or make fun of you. You may be afraid to make a mistake. Fear of failure can cause you not to try.

_____   **Fear of success**

You might be surprised to learn that some people fear success. Such people worry that they might lose friends if they are successful. Or they worry that they won't know who their real friends are. Some people fear success because they think it will turn them into workaholics. Others fear they aren't worthy of success. Fear of success can cause you to put things off, or it can make things turn out wrong.

_____ Fear of being hurt physically

You might fear that you are in physical danger, such as when you walk home alone at night. Or you might fear that if you take some action you will react with a physical stress reaction, such as your ulcer flaring up or breaking out in a rash. When you fear for your physical well-being, you try to avoid the situations that threaten you.

_____ Fear of being hurt emotionally

Some people feel afraid that they will lose a person who is important to them. Or they fear that they won't be able to cope with a situation. They worry that they might have a nervous breakdown or not be liked. If you have this type of fear, you try to please others and not risk your emotional well-being.

_____ Fear of the unknown

Many times you don't know what to expect. Things are uncertain. You don't know what will happen. You may feel out of control and afraid. When you fear the unknown, you don't want to take any risks. You want to play it safe and do things the way you have always done them.

Steps To Handle Fear

Fear is like any other emotion. You need to admit it to yourself before it will go away. After you recognize that you feel scared, you can do something about it. If you try to hide fear from yourself, you will probably express it as anger.

Here are the steps to follow to handle your feelings of fear:

Step 1: Notice when you feel afraid.
Don't try to hide the feeling from yourself. Many people first notice fear physically. Maybe you do, too. Do you notice butterflies in your stomach? Do your knees shake? Are you speechless?

Step 2: Make an action plan; take small steps.
Sometimes you scare yourself because what you want to do is so big. Break it down into small pieces. As you take the first step, and then the second, you will gain courage and confidence. You develop courage in the face of fear.

LIFT YOUR SPIRITS

RISKS

To laugh is to risk appearing the fool.
To weep is to risk appearing sentimental.
To reach out for another is to risk involvement.
To expose feelings is to risk exposing your true self.
To place your ideas, your dreams before a crowd is to risk their loss.
To love is to risk not being loved in return.
To live is to risk dying.
To hope is to risk despair.
To try is to risk failure.
But risks must be taken because the greatest hazard in life is to risk nothing.
The person who risks nothing does nothing, has nothing and is nothing.
They may avoid suffering and sorrow but they cannot learn, feel, change, grow, or live.
Chained by their certitudes they are a slave; they have forfeited their freedom.
Only a person who risks is free.

Anonymous, as quoted in <u>The Power of Purpose</u> by Dick Leider

Step 3: Remind yourself that you're growing.
When you feel afraid, it is a sign that you are stretching yourself. You are doing something new. You are growing! If you never felt fear, it would mean you weren't learning anything new.

Step 4: Celebrate your successes.
When you do something that scares you, congratulate yourself. Give yourself credit for taking a risk. Compliment your efforts. Step 4 will build your self-esteem and make the next risk easier to take.

✔ CHECKPOINT 9-4

YOUR GOAL:
Get 6 or more answers correct.

Write the word that will complete the following statements in the space provided. Choose your answer from the list of words provided. An example has been completed for you. Give yourself one point for each correct answer.

admit	failure	growing
physically	emotionally	steps
unknown	success	

● If you are afraid that if you do well you might lose your friends, you have fear of <u>success</u>.

1. People who worry about an ulcer flaring up or a heart attack fear being hurt _____.

2. If you are afraid that you will make a mistake or do something wrong, you have fear of _____.

3. You can handle your fears by breaking them into small _____.

4. Fear of the _____ is when you are uncertain about what will happen.

5. People who worry that they will be hurt _____ are afraid that they won't be liked, that they will embarass themselves, or that they will be rejected.

6. The first step to dealing with fear is to _____ it.

7. Fear is a sign that you are _____.

☞ *Check your work. Record your score.*

WHAT YOU HAVE LEARNED

Everyone has feelings. Feelings are not right or wrong, good or bad. What is important is how you choose to express your feelings. When you feel angry, there are four steps you can follow to express your anger and keep your self-esteem high. Feeling afraid is a sign that you are growing. There are four steps you can use to handle your fears. People with high self-esteem know how they feel and use their feelings to make wise choices.

ACTIVITY 9-1   **YOUR GOAL:** Get 10 points.

Read through the list of feelings in Illustration 9-1. Choose two feelings that you have felt. Write a brief paragraph about each feeling that describes when you felt it. Underline the feeling word that you are writing about in the paragraph. Give yourself five points for each paragraph. An example has been completed for you.

- One day I got a test back with an A on it. I was so proud of myself, and I couldn't wait to tell someone. The person I usually ride to school with was sick that day so I went home alone. When I got home, I called my best friend. No answer. I went next door to tell my neighbor, but he was too busy to talk. Finally I went back home. I felt so <u>lonely</u>. Good news and no one to tell.

1. _____

   _____

   _____

   _____

2. _____

   _____

   _____

   _____

☞ *Check your work. Record your score.*

ACTIVITY 9-2   **YOUR GOAL:** Get 4 or more answers correct.

Read each of the following statements. Put a *T* in the space provided if a statement is true. Put an *F* in the space provided if it is false. An example has been completed for you. Give yourself one point for each correct answer.

- __F__   You are controlled by your feelings.

1. _____   People with high self-esteem shut off unpleasant feelings.

2. _____   Different people may feel different things in the same situation.

3. _____   There is a right way and a wrong way to feel in most situations.

4. _____   The first step when you have a feeling is to admit it to yourself.

5. _____   Feelings that you hide from yourself can make you physically or emotionally sick.

☞ *Check your work. Record your score.*

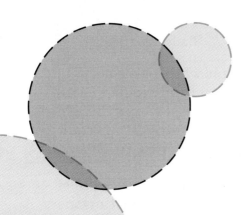

UNIT 10
KNOW YOUR VALUES

WHAT YOU WILL LEARN

When you finish this unit, you will be able to:

- Identify your values and their source.
- Identify at least two reasons why people don't live their values.
- Stop value judging.

You have a personal code that you use to decide what is right and what is wrong. This code is your values. Different people have different values. How you behave is one clue to what you value.

For example, if the clerk at the store gave you too much change and you gave it back to him, it would suggest that you value honesty. If a co-worker asked you to clock in for her and you said "no," it would reinforce that you value honesty. If a friend asked you to come over and you were tired and told him the truth, it would be another example of honesty. When you put all of these behaviors together, you come to the conclusion that honesty is one of your values. People probably call you an "honest person."

WHERE DID YOU GET YOUR VALUES?

Your values are formed during the first ten to twelve years of life. You learn your values from other people. You watch what they say and do. You use what you observe to decide what is "normal" and how to behave. Your ideas today about right and wrong are based on what you learned about the world when you were a child.

If you grew up in a family where you were hugged and kissed and told "I love you," that's what you will think is normal. If you grew up in a family where you were yelled at and hit, that's what you will think is normal. What you think is normal is often what you think is "right."

One source of values, then, is the people who raised you. You use them as a model to understand the world and decide what is right and wrong. They are not the only source of values though. You also learn about what is important and what isn't important from teachers at school, your religion, your friends, neighbors, movies, and television.

In the past, parents or guardians were the major source of values. Children spent more time with these people than anyone else. Today that has changed. Many children live in single-parent homes, and the parent works outside the home. A child may spend more time with the television than any person. The television becomes the major source of values. The child learns the right way to live from the commercials and programs he or she watches.

Current events are the background that shape each generation's values. People who grow up at the same time often share some common values. This is because they were exposed to similar experiences. Examples of events that shaped values are shown in Illustration 10-1.

Growing Up in the 60s

People who grew up during the 1960s were exposed to the Vietnam War, hippies, the Civil Rights Movement, and the Women's Movement. These experiences shaped their values. Today you find that people who grew up during the 60s are still concerned about social justice.

Growing Up in the 70s

People who grew up during the 1970s had different experiences that shaped their values. They watched President Nixon resign, saw oil prices go up, and saw long lines form at gasoline stations. They were part of the "Me Generation" and saw women enter the labor force in record numbers. Today these people are concerned that there won't be enough for them to get their fair share.

Growing Up in the 80s

Those who grew up during the 1980s witnessed a decade of greed. The heroes were people like Donald Trump. Image was very important. The country was run on borrowed money creating the largest deficit in history. The stock market had the biggest fall since the Great Depression. Hanging over people's heads was the threat of nuclear war and the destruction of the natural environment. What values do you think the ten-year olds of the 80s will bring into adulthood?

Illustration 10-1

Three Decades
in Pictures

The 60's—The Vietnam
War

The 70s—Gas Lines

The 80s—Recycling

CHECKPOINT 10-1

Read the following list of values. Rate each value on a scale of 1-10, with 10 being extremely important to you and 1 being unimportant to you. Write out your five most important values in the space provided. An example has been completed for you. Give yourself ten points for completing the Checkpoint.

Value	Rating	Value	Rating
● achievement	9		
1. achievement		15. personal growth	
2. appearance		16. physical health	
3. arts		17. pleasure	
4. career		18. power	
5. creativity		19. privacy	
6. environment		20. recognition	
7. family		21. relationships	
8. honesty		22. religion	
9. learning		23. risk taking	
10. leisure		24. security	
11. love		25. service	
12. loyalty		26. socializing	
13. meaning		27. spiritual	
14. money		28. status	

My top five values:

1. _____
2. _____
3. _____
4. _____
5. _____

☞ *Check your work. Record your score.*

IT'S HARD TO LIVE YOUR VALUES

Sadly, many people don't live according to their values because it is hard to do. Doing the "right" thing is not the same as doing the easy thing. It takes discipline to put your values into practice.

Perhaps you value your physical health. You want a strong, healthy body. You might decide to eat less sugar and to start an exercise program. For the first few days you follow the plan you set for yourself. Then one evening when you come home from work you feel tired. You don't feel like exercising, and you don't. The next day a friend offers you a piece of birthday cake, and you accept. Now your behavior is in conflict with your values. What will you do?

If you do what is easiest (stop exercising and eat sweets), you will lower your self-esteem. Why? Because you aren't doing what you believe is "right." You aren't living up to your values. If you don't live according to your personal code, you will have trouble respecting yourself. How can you like yourself — have high self-esteem — if you don't respect yourself?

Your second choice is to remind yourself that you aren't perfect. You slipped. You still value your health and want to make healthy choices. You re-commit to your goal and start again. This builds your self-esteem.

✔ CHECKPOINT 10-2

YOUR GOAL:
Get 10 points.

Read through the following list of values. Rate your behavior on a scale of 1 to 10 for each value. If your behavior reflects the value, put a 10 in the space provided. If your behavior does not reflect the value, put a 1 in the space provided. An example has been completed for you. Compare how you rated each value in Checkpoint 10-1 with how you rate your behavior in this Checkpoint. Do the two match? Give yourself ten points for rating your behavior on each of the values.

Value	Behavior	Value	Behavior
● achievement	8		
1. achievement	_____	15. personal growth	_____
2. appearance	_____	16. physical health	_____
3. arts	_____	17. pleasure	_____
4. career	_____	18. power	_____
5. creativity	_____	19. privacy	_____
6. environment	_____	20. recognition	_____
7. family	_____	21. relationships	_____
8. honesty	_____	22. religion	_____
9. learning	_____	23. risk taking	_____
10. leisure	_____	24. security	_____
11. love	_____	25. service	_____
12. loyalty	_____	26. socializing	_____
13. meaning	_____	27. spiritual	_____
14. money	_____	28. status	_____

☞ *Check your work. Record your score.*

You may have discovered in the preceding exercise that your behavior does not agree with what you say is important. Do you need to make some changes in your behavior so that there is a better match? When your values and your behavior agree, you like yourself more. You have high self-esteem.

When Values Change

When your behavior and your values don't match, you may need to evaluate your values. Perhaps your physical health isn't as important as you thought. You might decide that pleasure is more important than health. Then you can eat the cake and skip the exercise without feeling guilty or damaging your self-esteem.

Most people do not change their values easily, however. Because your values were formed when you were young, you rarely question them. Usually, you need a significant emotional experience before you will change your values.

For example, you may have grown up with a value that marriage is forever and divorce is wrong. If there was conflict in your marriage, you would cope with it the best you could because of your values about marriage. But, if your partner became physically abusive, you might decide that your values are outdated. They don't cover this special situation. Being battered could be a significant emotional experience that causes you to change your values. You might decide that divorce is okay in this situation.

LIFT YOUR SPIRITS

There are holidays for almost everything — Valentine's Day, birthdays, Mother's Day, Father's Day, Grandparents' Day, Boss's Day, Secretaries' Day. But what about our friends? When do we take the time to celebrate the friendships we have? Make a list of your best friends. Then decide how you can let them know how important they are to you.

From time to time it is important to review your values. Do they still fit? Do they make sense for your life? Or do they need to be changed, or updated? For example, many people are changing their values about the environment. They recycle now. They try not to waste resources. For most people this is a new value that fits a changing world. The preceding Checkpoints are an excellent tool to help you re-think your values.

When Values Conflict

A **value conflict** occurs when two values compete with each other. You cannot honor both values at the same time. You are forced to decide which of the two values is most important. These are usually difficult decisions. Let's look at some examples.

Example 1:

Imagine that you value education. You want to do well in school and you study hard. You also value your family. It is important to you to spend time with your children and do things together. You have a test coming up in one of your classes the same night as your son's big game of the season. He wants you to be at the game. What do you do?

Example 2:

Imagine that relationships are very important to you. You want to have friends and be liked by them. When you were growing up, you watched your mother battle alcoholism. You have decided not to drink. Your friends want you to join them at a local bar after work for a few drinks. What do you do?

Example 3:

Imagine you are supporting a family by yourself. It is hard to make ends meet. You have a chance for a promotion that means more money. The person who will be your new boss has made racist comments to other people in the department. If you take this job, you will likely be the next target. You are proud of your heritage, and you don't think it is right to accept racist treatment. You also want to provide for your family. What do you do?

There is no "right" answer to the preceding dilemmas. There is only *your* answer, based on your values. In value conflict situations, you are forced to rank order your values and decide which one is the most important to you. Whatever you decide, you may feel some pain about not being able to honor both values equally.

✓ CHECKPOINT 10-3

YOUR GOAL:
Get 15 points.

Read each of the following value conflict situations. Decide what you would do. Write your answer in the space provided. An example has been completed for you. Give yourself five points for each answer.

- Your son wants you to attend his basketball game the same night you have a test at school. What would you do?

  Take the test because it will help our future. I would

  explain my decision to my son and try to make plans for us

  to do something else another time.

1. Your best friend is going to court and has asked you to testify for her. If you tell the truth, your friend will be in trouble. If you lie, you will break your oath to tell the truth, and you might get in trouble. What would you do?

   _____

   _____

2. You are hungry and you have no money. When you go into a store, you see that you could take something to eat and no one would see you. What would you do?

   _____

   _____

3. You see a co-worker steal something from the company. A few days later management starts asking questions. What would you do?

   _____

   _____

☞ *Check your work. Record your score.*

STOP VALUE JUDGING

There may be another reason that you aren't living your values. You may have rated some of the values high in Checkpoint 10-1 because you thought you "should." You may have completed the value rating the way you think a parent or instructor would. Or you may have rated a value the way you think society would rank it. If that happened, these aren't your values, they're shoulds in disguise as your values!

If the values you rated high were really shoulds, then you were value judging. **Value judging** is applying someone else's values to your life and judging yourself according to them. Because they aren't your values, you will probably come up short. You'll feel bad about yourself. You'll lower your self-esteem.

Here's an example. American society has put a high value on money. Many people believe that having money is important. Some people will use the amount of money you make to judge you. If you have money, you are judged "okay." If you don't have money, you are judged "not okay."

But what if your highest value is relationships and service to others? You may be rich in friendships. If you judge yourself according to someone else's values — in this case the amount of money you make — you will feel low self-esteem. You will get caught by shoulds and others' expectations instead of living your life according to what you believe is right. You will live your life from the outside in, instead of from the inside out.

If you refuse to judge yourself by someone else's standards, your self-esteem will stay high. You know what your values are. You know what is important to you in your life. Use *your* values to guide your behavior, and you will like yourself.

There is one more important point. If you don't judge yourself by others' values, then you can't judge others by your values. You need to learn to disagree without judging. You need to observe, not judge differences.

For example, you may value relationships, and your brother may value achievement. Don't judge him for working long hours when you prefer to be with your family. You each make your choices based on your values. It is okay to have different values.

The key to high self-esteem is to stop value judging. Accept yourself as you are. Accept other people as they are. Stop value judging yourself and stop value judging others. See differences as the gift that makes every person unique. Don't see differences as something to be destroyed and replaced with sameness. Don't judge differences as right or wrong, good or bad. Appreciate differences for the richness they bring to life.

When you meet someone who is different, try to understand him or her. Use your communication skills to listen, ask questions, and see the world from a new viewpoint. Understanding instead of judging others will raise your self-esteem and the self-esteem of others.

CHECKPOINT 10-4

YOUR GOAL:
Get 4 or more answers correct.

Answer each of the following questions in the space provided. An example has been completed for you. Give yourself one point for each correct answer.

● What is value judging?

   <u>Value judging is applying someone else's values to</u>

   <u>your life and judging yourself according to them.</u>

1. Why are some values really shoulds?

   _____

   _____

2. What happens if you value judge?

   _____

   _____

3. What is the opposite of value judging?

   _____

   _____

4. What do you do if someone you care about has different values than you?

   _____

   _____

5. What is the key to high self-esteem?

   _____

   _____

☞ *Check your work. Record your score.*

Now you have all the skills you need to stop judging yourself. It's up to you to put them to use. When you do, you'll find that you can say "I like myself!" and mean it. Good luck.

WHAT YOU HAVE LEARNED

Every person has a set of values that they use to decide the right and wrong way to live. You got your values from the important people around you when you grew up, current events, movies, and television. It is hard to live your values. Sometimes values conflict, and you are faced with hard choices. You may need to change your values at times. The key to high self-esteem is to know your values and not value judge.

ACTIVITY 10-1   YOUR GOAL: Get 8 or more answers correct.

Read each of the following statements. Put a *T* in the space provided if a statement is true. Put an *F* in the space provided if it is false. Give yourself one point for each correct answer. An example has been completed for you.

-    __F__   Parents are the only source of your values.

1. _____   Your values are set by the time you are ten or twelve years old.

2. _____   People who grow up during the same time period often have similar values.

3. _____   Television does not affect your values.

4. _____   The best way to tell a person's values is to ask her or him.

5. _____   A value conflict is when you and another person disagree about what is right.

6. _____   To solve a value conflict, you rank order your values.

7. _____   When you value judge, you raise your self-esteem.

8. _____   Sometimes what we think are our values are really someone else's shoulds.

9. _____   To live your life according to your values is one way to build high self-esteem.

10. _____   It is easy to live your values.

☞ *Check your work. Record your score.*

ACTIVITY 10-2   YOUR GOAL: Get 20 points.

Write a two- or three-paragraph essay about your values. Describe what is most important to you and why. Tell where you got these values. Give examples of how you express your values in your everyday life. Tell why it is sometimes hard to live your values. Give yourself twenty points for your essay.

_____

_____

_____

_____

_____

_____

_____

_____

_____

_____

_____

_____

_____

_____

☞ *Check your work. Record your score.*

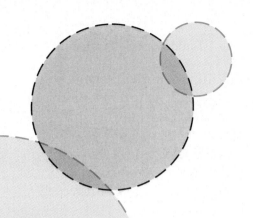

UNIT 11
POSITIVE SELF-TALK

WHAT YOU WILL LEARN

When you finish this unit, you will be able to:

- Create your own Fan Club.
- Write an affirmation.

As you've learned, the Judge uses negative self-talk to keep your self-esteem low. In this Unit, you are going to meet your Fan Club and learn how to use positive self-talk.

MEET YOUR FAN CLUB

What is a Fan Club? It's a group of people who believe in you 100 percent. In their eyes, you can do no wrong. They're proud of your every achievement, no matter how big or small. According to your Fan Club, if you face a disappointment, it's because there's something better waiting for you. When you feel uncertain, your Fan Club encourages you. When life feels hard, your Fan Club reminds you how much you're learning. They are a very positive group, as you can see in Illustration 11-1. They are with you all the time to help you love yourself and be the best you can be.

Illustration 11-1

Your Fan Club

Each person has a Fan Club inside of him or herself. Sometimes you're so busy listening to the Judge that you don't pay attention to your Fan Club. Who you listen to—the Judge or your Fan Club--controls your level of self-esteem.

Who are the members of your Fan Club? You decide. There is only one test to pass to be in your Fan Club. *Does he or she believe in you?* A Fan Club is no place for someone who doesn't believe that you are wonderful!

Some people have their mother, father, or both in their Fan Club. Other people have a favorite instructor. Many people have Jesus or God in their Fan Club. Friends, children, bosses, and co-workers have been found in Fan Clubs. Even pets have been included. You can have as many people (or animals!) as you want in your Fan Club.

Stop now and think about who is in your Fan Club. Don't forget yourself, either! You can root for you! Write down the names of the people in your Fan Club in the space provided.

My Fan Club:

_____

_____

_____

Anytime you feel down, you can ask your Fan Club to cheer you. Anytime the Judge starts talking to you, you can decide to listen to your Fan Club instead. You aren't alone. Your Fan Club is on your side.

START USING AFFIRMATIONS

Your Fan Club uses a special kind of self-talk called affirmations. An **affirmation** is a positive statement you say to yourself that builds you up, rather than tearing you down. An affirmation is a way of talking to yourself that says you count. You're important. You're okay.

An affirmation has four key characteristics: it is positive, said in the present tense, visualized, and repeated often. If any one of the characteristics is missing, the affirmation is not as powerful. Let's look at each of the parts in turn.

An Affirmation Is Positive

You might be thinking to yourself, "Well of course!" But it is not as easy as it sounds. For an affirmation to be positive, it needs to say what you *want*, not what you *don't* want.

Look at the following example Rick wrote:
"I don't want to get sick."

◄ **LIFT YOUR SPIRITS**

There is a well-known children's story about the Little Engine That Could. In the story, a little engine needs to pull a heavy load over a mountain. He used affirmations. He first told himself, "I think I can, I think I can." Then he said "I know I can, I know I can." The next time you face a hard task, remember the words of The Little Engine That Could.

He thought this was a positive statement. It's not a negative statement, but it doesn't meet the rule to be a positive statement, either. "I don't want to get sick," tells us what Rick *doesn't* want, but we don't know what he *does* want. Here's how he could re-write it to be positive:

"I am healthy."

You may know what you don't like or don't want. It is much harder to know what you *do* like and want. Your Fan Club needs to know specifically how to cheer you on. They get excited about saying, "Rick is healthy!" They don't think "Rick doesn't want to get sick" is motivating.

The key to making your affirmation positive is avoiding the word *not*. Watch out for do not (don't) and will not (won't). Replace these words with what you want.

Here's another example: "I don't make mistakes." Do you see the problem for your Fan Club? They don't know what this means. It isn't positive. To make it a powerful affirmation, take out the "don't." Decide what you want. One way to change it would be to say, "I get A's on my math tests." Another affirmation might be, "I check my work." Each of the last two examples are positive. They say what you want.

✔ **CHECKPOINT 11-1**

YOUR GOAL:
Get 5 answers correct.

Read each of the following statements. Decide if they meet the first step to be an affirmation. Write *yes* in the space provided if a statement is positive. Write *no* if it is not. An example has been completed for you. Give yourself one point for each correct answer.

●   <u> no </u>   I don't waste time.

1.   <u>   </u>   I manage my time.

2.   <u>   </u>   I don't owe anyone any money.

3.   <u>   </u>   I won't be late.

4.   <u>   </u>   I'm not lonely.

5. _____   I love my job.

6. _____   I'm not scared.

☞ *Check your work. Record your score.*

An Affirmation Uses the Present Tense

The second characteristic of an affirmation is that it is said in the present tense. Not the past tense. Not the future tense. Say it as if it is true NOW. Today.

Stating an affirmation as if it's true is hard for some people to do. If it isn't true yet, it seems like you are lying to yourself. What you're really doing is using a special feature of the mind.

By stating your affirmation as if it is true right now, you give yourself courage to do something today to make it true. You start to think about yourself in a different way. After all, when you use negative self-talk, don't you put it in the present tense? Don't you say things to yourself like, "I'm so stupid," rather than, "I'm going to be stupid." You know how powerful the negative self-talk is. You're applying the same rules to your positive self-talk. So instead of saying, "I will have confidence," say, "I have confidence." Here are more examples:

FUTURE TENSE	PRESENT TENSE
I will do a good job.	I do a good job.
I will pay the bills on time.	I pay the bills on time.

The point is, you want to affirm to yourself what you want, as if it is true today. Put your affirmations in the present tense. Decide to believe them. This sets in motion all kinds of mental processes that will make them come true.

✔ CHECKPOINT 11-2

YOUR GOAL:
Get 5 answers correct.

Rewrite the following affirmations so that they are in the present tense. An example has been completed for you. Give yourself one point for each correct answer.

● I will get healthy.
  I am healthy. _____

1. I will lose weight.

   _____

2. I will pass the test.

   _____

3. I will get a new job.

_____

4. I will study for the next test.

_____

5. I will read to the kids before they go to bed.

_____

☞ *Check your work. Record your score.*

Visualize Your Affirmation

When you **visualize** something, you see a picture of it in your mind. You make pictures in your mind all day long. Everybody does. When you talk to someone, you "see" what they say. When you think about something, you often "see" what you're thinking about. Few people realize that you can also visualize high self-esteem!

To explain how you can use visualization to raise your self-esteem, you need to understand how the mind works. The mind is an amazing tool. Yet, it cannot tell the difference between imagination and reality.

Try this experiment. Imagine walking into your kitchen. You pick up a large yellow lemon. Feel the slightly rough texture of the skin against your hands. Now, get a paring knife and cut the lemon in half. Notice how juicy the lemon is as you cut it. In fact, it squirts you! Now smell the fresh, clean smell of the lemon. Bring half of the lemon up towards your nose. Breathe in. Doesn't it smell good? Now, take a big bite of the lemon. Sink your teeth into the fruit....

What is happening in your mouth right now? Is it watering? If so, you might wonder why. You aren't eating a lemon. Or are you? In your mind you are. Your mind reacts to anything it can picture clearly, and in detail, as if it is real. That's why you can salivate just thinking about eating a lemon.

If it can work with a lemon, why not make it work for your self-esteem? Maybe you've been picturing yourself as not being very lovable. Maybe you've pictured yourself as a poor student. Maybe

LIFT YOUR SPIRITS

An American pilot was a prisoner of war (POW) in North Vietnam for many years. He lost 80 pounds and much of his health while he was a POW. When he came home, one of the first things he wanted to do was play a game of golf. He played a great game. No one could understand it because he was so thin and he hadn't played in years. He told them that while in prison he visualized himself playing golf every day.

you've pictured yourself in a job you don't like. These are the negative pictures that come from the Judge. The Judge doesn't paint pretty pictures in your mind. But because the pictures seem so real, *you act as if they are true*. Then you feel bad about yourself and have low self-esteem.

You can change the pictures! Instead of listening to the Judge, listen to your Fan Club. Start creating some new pictures in your mind. Your life won't change overnight, but it will start to change. You can start visualizing yourself today as the kind of person you want to be. Replace the old pictures with new, positive ones. Listen to your Fan Club. "See" what they have to say to you. You can choose which inner voice you will listen to. You can decide who will be in charge of your life — the Judge, or your Fan Club. It's up to you.

This is an important point. *What you see is what you get.* Until you can see yourself in the kind of job you want in your mind's eye, you won't get the kind of job you want. Until you can see yourself as a confident person in your mind, you won't be a confident person. Until you can see yourself having friends in your mind, you won't have friends. Be careful about the movies that you watch in your mind! They affect how you feel about yourself. They affect who you are.

✔ CHECKPOINT 11-3

YOUR GOAL:
Get 10 points.

Think about the way the Judge talks to you. Write a paragraph about the person you picture when you listen to the Judge. Then think about your Fan Club. Write a paragraph about the person you picture when you listen to your Fan Club. An example has been completed for you. Give yourself five points for each paragraph.

● Who do you see when you listen to the Judge?

I see a person who can't do anything right, so she doesn't

try new things. People laugh at her. She doesn't like

herself. She feels inadequate most of the time.

Who do you see when you listen to your Fan Club?

I see a confident person who can do anything she decides

to do. She takes risks, has friends, and feels happy. She

learns new things.

a. Who do you see when you listen to the Judge?

_____

_____

_____

_____

b. Who do you see when you listen to your Fan Club?

_____

_____

_____

_____

☞ *Check your work. Record your score.*

Say Your Affirmations Often

Self-talk goes on all the time. In the past, you have listened to the Judge most of the time. Now it is time to listen to your Fan Club.

Here's how you do it. First, when the Judge starts talking, decide you aren't going to listen. Talk back to the Judge with words from your Fan Club. It is a good idea to have some phrases in mind that you can use. For example, you could say one of these statements to the Judge:

I like myself.
I am special.
I am somebody.
I count.
I am important.

Second, pick two or three affirmations that you will say to yourself every morning when you get up and every night before you go to bed. You can also say the affirmations to yourself during the day. Think of these as being self-esteem food. Each day you eat food to keep your body physically fit. You know that if you eat too many sweets, drink too much, or skip meals, your body doesn't feel good. You need to give it healthy food so it can do it's best.

You also need to feed your self-esteem. If the only food it gets is from the Judge, you won't feel good about yourself. Decide to feed your self-esteem at least twice a day. Here are some examples of affirmations that you can use.

I love and accept myself.
I'm getting better and better everyday.
I now release all comparisons with others.
I am at peace.

I love and appreciate all of my natural abilities.
I let go of negative thoughts.
I am a loving person.

You don't need to feel limited to these affirmations. You can write your own. You now know all the parts to include.

✔ CHECKPOINT 11-4

YOUR GOAL:
Get 4 or more points.

Write two affirmations you can use when the Judge starts to talk to you. Then write two affirmations that you can use each day to build your self esteem. Review the last section for examples. Give yourself two points for each one you write.

Affirmation 1: _____

_____

Affirmation 2: _____

_____

Affirmation 3: _____

_____

Affirmation 4: _____

_____

☞ *Check your work. Record your score.*

Keep your affirmations short. You want to be able to remember them! Don't try to say too many of them at one time. It works best to choose two or three that you will say to yourself each day. Begin by using affirmations to raise your self-esteem. As you succeed in that area, you can start using affirmations in other parts of your life. There is no limit to their possible use.

Affirmations are a tool you can use to change your life. Test their power by using them every day for thirty days. You'll like what you discover.

WHAT YOU HAVE LEARNED

You have a Fan Club! You can choose to listen to the Judge and lower your self-esteem. Or you can listen to your Fan Club and build your self-esteem. Your Fan Club will talk to you in affirmations. To be most powerful, an affirmation is positive, said in the present tense, visualized, and used often.

ACTIVITY 11-1   **YOUR GOAL:** Get 6 or more points.

Answer the following questions in the space provided. An example has been completed for you. Give yourself two points for each answer.

● What is a Fan Club?

  <u>A group of people in your mind who believe in you. They cheer you on</u>

  <u>and talk positively to you.</u>

1. Name and explain the first part of an affirmation.

  _____

  _____

  _____

2. Name and explain the second part of an affirmation.

  _____

  _____

  _____

3. Name and explain the third part of an affirmation.

  _____

  _____

  _____

4. Name and explain the fourth part of an affirmation.

  _____

  _____

  _____

☞ *Check your work. Record your score.*

ACTIVITY 11-2   YOUR GOAL: Get 8 or more answers correct.

The following statements are not affirmations as written. Why not? Write the reason in the space provided. An example has been completed for you. Give yourself one point for each correct answer.

● I don't do well on tests.

    _____Negative_____

1. I won't be chosen for the job.

    _____

2. I will learn to accept myself.

    _____

3. I won't get any help.

    _____

4. I wish I could read better.

    _____

5. I will stand up for myself.

    _____

6. I don't do well in job interviews.

    _____

7. I won't be liked.

    _____

8. I won't lose my keys.

    _____

9. I won't be turned down for the raise.

    _____

10. I will be happy.

    _____

☞ *Check your work. Record your score.*

UNIT 12
I LIKE MYSELF!

WHAT YOU WILL LEARN

When you finish this unit, you will be able to:

- Keep your self-esteem high.
- Build the self-esteem of others by affirming others.
- Set SMART goals.

Liking yourself is a lifetime job. Once you have mastered the ideas in this book to build your self-esteem, you aren't done. Your high self-esteem needs to be maintained.

MAINTAIN HIGH SELF-ESTEEM

From time to time your self-esteem will slip. Your self-esteem is like a yo-yo. It goes up and down. You want to keep it high as much as you can. Here are some tips to maintain high self-esteem.

Spend Time With Positive People

As you've learned, other people can help you build your self-esteem. Positive people can also help you maintain your self-esteem.

You decide who your friends are. Choose people who believe in you, like in Illustration 12-1. Choose people who look for the positive in even a negative situation. On days when you feel your self-esteem is low, call one of these people to lift your spirits.

Stop spending time with people who bring you down. At work, take breaks and eat lunch with positive people. Your self-esteem is too important to let anyone damage it. You may need to change some of your relationships to keep your self-esteem high.

Illustration 12-1

A Friend Believes in You

Look To The Future, Not The Past

Anyone can look back and see a better way to do things. It is easy to get stuck thinking about what "could have been" or "should have been." The problem with this type of thinking is that you can't change the past.

However, you can *learn* from your past. You can use the past to change how you act in the future. You can keep your self-esteem high if you use today to make a better tomorrow. Accept that you are a developing human being. Each mistake is a chance to learn. When things don't turn out the way you had hoped, decide how you will do it differently the next time.

Keep yourself focused on the future, when you can change your behavior. Notice the difference in the following examples between looking back and looking forward.

PAST: "I judged myself again. I should have accepted my mistake. I just can't get it right."

FUTURE: "I realize I made myself feel bad when I judged myself. Next time I will describe the situation instead of judge it."

PAST: "I don't know why I didn't speak up when my supervisor asked me to work late. I could have saved myself a lot of problems if I would have said how I felt."

FUTURE: "I notice I didn't speak up. It is still hard for me to express my feelings. I'm going to practice saying what I feel so I'm not in this situation again."

PAST: "I feel so awful about yelling at the kids. I shouldn't have said the things I said to them."

FUTURE: "I lost control of my feelings with the kids. Next time I feel mad I'm going to send them to their room until I cool off."

In each example, the first statement judged the past and caused feelings of low self-esteem. There is no way to change the situation or fix the problem. You are stuck when you look back. The second statement looks to the future with a plan to do better. Describe your past with a focus on what you will change in the future.

✓ CHECKPOINT 12-1

YOUR GOAL: Get 4 or more answers correct.

Read each of the following statements. Decide if each looks to the past or the future. Write *past* or *future* in the space provided. An example has been completed for you. Give yourself one point for each correct answer.

- ●   __past__   I shouldn't have said that.
1. _____   Why did I spend money on those magazines?
2. _____   Next month I'll make a budget so I don't run short on money.
3. _____   Next time I buy a new appliance I'll ask more questions.
4. _____   I knew I should have brought an umbrella.
5. _____   If I'd left earlier I wouldn't be running late.

☞ *Check your work. Record your score.*

Accept Yourself

No one can be a better YOU than you! If you try to be someone else, you will fail. And you will lower your self-esteem in the process. The world needs *you* to be *you*. No one else can do it. On the days when you feel your self-esteem starting to slip, say to yourself, "I am me. There is no one else quite like me. I will be the best me that I can be."

You may set goals to develop yourself. That doesn't change the fact that you are okay today as you are. You don't criticize a seed because it isn't a tree yet. Accept yourself. Like a seed, you have lots of growing to do. That's normal. Everyone needs to grow and develop him or herself. Your life is a process of becoming the best you can be. Accepting yourself as you are now, today, makes it possible for you to grow and develop. When you feel okay about yourself, you are able to risk change.

Do Something You Love

You are like a battery. You have energy that you give to others all day long. Like a battery, you sometimes need to be recharged. Being with positive friends is one way to charge your battery. Another way is to do something you love to do.

What do you love to do? Make a list of ten things right now. Put things on your list that you can do alone, and things you can do with a friend. List things you can do for free, as well as things that cost money.

Things I love to do:

_____

_____

_____

_____

How often do you do the things you love? Look at this list when your self-esteem slips. Then choose something from the list to do to give your self-esteem a lift.

✔ CHECKPOINT 12-2

YOUR GOAL:
Get 4 or more answers correct.

Read each of the following statements. If a statement is true, put a *T* in the space provided. If it is false, put an *F* in the space provided. An example has been completed for you. Give yourself one point for each correct answer.

- ___F___   If your self-esteem slips, there's nothing you can do about it.
1. _____   If you have a hard day, it can help to spend time with positive people.
2. _____   You will feel better about yourself if you try to be like someone else who has high self-esteem.
3. _____   Most people who look back into the past see things they wish they had or hadn't done. This lowers self-esteem.
4. _____   You can lower your self-esteem by doing things you love.
5. _____   The keys to maintaining high self-esteem are to be around positive people, look to the future, be yourself, and do things you love.

☞ *Check your work. Record your score.*

AFFIRM OTHERS

You are not alone in wanting high self-esteem. Everyone wants to like him or herself. As you start to affirm yourself, you'll find that it feels natural to affirm others, too.

Notice What People Do That You Like

So often we look for what people do wrong. That is the Judge inside who wants to criticize. As you listen more to your Fan Club and less to your Judge, you'll notice that you don't judge yourself *or others* as often.

Look for what people do right. Don't look for big things. Look for the little things. The coworker who greets you with a smile. The friend who listens to you. The family member who helps out. The neighbor who lets you get on the bus first. The stranger who holds a door open for you. These small kindnesses make a difference in your life.

As you put your attention on these gestures of goodwill, you will notice more and more of them. The world will seem a nicer place. Nothing has changed, except your attitude.

Say Thank You

Take a minute to say "Thank you" when someone does something you like. The more specific you can be, the more it will mean to the other person. When you are specific, the person knows exactly what you liked. They don't have to guess. For example, "Thanks for your help" doesn't say as much as "Thank you for helping me fold the sheets."

Another way to say thanks is to use the words "I appreciate." Again, follow the words with as much detail as possible. "I appreciate your thoughtfulness" doesn't mean as much as "I appreciate you calling to ask how my Dad is feeling." When you are specific, the other person knows that you noticed. A "Thank you" or "I appreciate. . . ." builds self-esteem in others. When they know you noticed, they are more likely to do the same thing again. That's good for both of you!

Don't Judge Others

It is so easy to judge others. This hurts your self-esteem and their self-esteem. As long as you judge others, it is a sign that you are judging yourself. Here are some things to avoid.

Don't put others down. How will a put-down help you or the other person? It won't. When you feel good about yourself at someone else's expense, it is a sign of low self-esteem. Instead of putting others down, challenge yourself to find something to appreciate. You'll both feel better.

Don't gossip. If you hear gossip, let it stop with you. Don't pass it on. If someone wants to talk behind another person's back, say, "I don't want to hear it."

LIFT YOUR SPIRITS

"If the only prayer you ever say is Thank You, it's enough."

Meister Eckhart

Don't laugh at sexist or racist jokes. Those types of jokes come from low self-esteem and comparisons. If you won't be an audience, the jokes will stop.

Don't take advantage of people with low self-esteem. Be a person who helps them build their self-esteem.

CHECKPOINT 12-3

YOUR GOAL:
Get 4 or more answers correct.

Read each of the following situations. Decide how you would respond to build self-esteem in another. Write your answer in the space provided. An example has been completed for you. Give yourself one point for each correct answer.

- When it was raining your spouse said, "You wait here. I'll get the car and pick you up."

  <u>I appreciate you bringing the car to pick me up so I didn't</u>
  <u>get wet.</u>

1. A co-worker wants to tell you about the trouble Kelly is in.

   _____

   _____

2. You're with a group of friends after work, and they start to tell sexist and racist jokes.

   _____

   _____

3. April brings you a can of fruit juice at break time.

   _____

   _____

4. You call a store about the price of an item. The person who answers the phone is friendly and gets you an answer quickly.

   _____

   _____

5. You have a doctor appointment at 2:00 p.m. The doctor's office calls you at 1:15 to say the doctor is running late and asks if you can come at 2:30 p.m.

   _____

   _____

☞ *Check your work. Record your score.*

SET SMART GOALS

You have learned many things that will help you build your self-esteem. Once you decide which ideas you want to use, you need to set goals and take action. Knowledge without action is like a car without gas. You won't get too far.

Most people don't set goals. Of the ones who do, few know how to set a goal so that they will reach it. If the only idea you get from this book is to set goals — and you do — your life will make a change for the better.

All you need to remember is to set SMART goals. Here's what SMART stands for:

S - SPECIFIC
M - MEASURABLE
A - ACHIEVABLE
R - REALISTIC
T - TIMEBOUND

Be Specific

You want your goal to be as clear as possible. Then you know what you want to achieve. If a goal is vague, or too general, it won't help you get what you want.

For example, if you had the goal, "Lose Weight," it wouldn't work well. Why not? It isn't specific. To make the goal specific, you could say, "I want to lose ten pounds." Here are some other examples.

VAGUE	SPECIFIC
Be a better parent.	Read to my child fifteen minutes each night.
Get better grades.	Earn a B in math class.
Have a nice car.	Drive a car with no rust on the body.
Look better.	Get a new hairstyle.

If the goal isn't specific, you don't have a way to tell if you are meeting it or not. If you can't measure your progress, you will probably drop the goal.

LIFT YOUR SPIRITS

A visitor was watching two stonemasons work. He went up to the first stonemason and asked what he was doing. The reply was, "I'm cutting stone." Then the visitor went up to the second stonemason and asked the same question. The reply was, "I'm building a cathedral." Which stonemason had a goal? Do you have goals?

Make Goals Measurable ━━━━━━━━━━━

You need to know if you are meeting your goals. You need a way to measure them. If you can't tell if you are reaching them, why set them?

You can't measure a goal that is vague. Look at the preceding examples of goals. How would you know if you were a better parent? There is no way to tell. But would you know if you read to your child fifteen minutes each night? Yes. That is a measurable goal. Would you know when you lost 10 pounds? Yes. Could you tell if you got a new hairstyle? Yes. A specific goal will give you a way to measure your progress. You will know when you reach the goal. When you do, you can celebrate.

Be sure you have the means to measure your goal. For example, you can measure weight loss with a scale. But do you have a scale? If not, the goal isn't measurable for you. You might need to change it to say, "Fit into a size 10 dress," if you are a woman. Or "Wear pants with a 38-inch waist," if you are a man. You could measure your dress or waist size when you go to the store to buy clothes. It isn't enough that the goal can be measured. *You* need to be able to measure the goal.

✔ CHECKPOINT 12-4

YOUR GOAL:
Get 4 or more answers correct.

Read each of the following goals. Decide if each goal is specific and measurable. If it is, write *yes* in the space provided. If it isn't write *no*. An example has been completed for you. Give yourself one point for each correct answer.

● ___yes___ Pay all of my bills on the day they are due or earlier.

1. _____ Get a better job.

2. _____ Get married.

3. _____ Spend more time with friends.

4. _____ Watch less TV.

5. _____ Get up when the alarm goes off.

☞ *Check your work. Record your score.*

Is Your Goal Achievable? ━━━━━━━━━

The preceding question is very important if you tend to be a perfectionist. Has what you want to do ever been done before? Is it possible? Do you know how to do it? Some perfectionists set goals for themselves that aren't achievable. Then, when they don't achieve the goal, they feel bad about themselves.

You may decide that your goal is achievable, but you need to reach some other goals first. For example, it may be achievable for you to read to your child, but you may need to develop your reading skills first.

Is Your Goal Realistic?

Being realistic about your goal is important, too. You need to know yourself well enough to know what you can and can't do. There are many goals that are achievable, yet *unrealistic* for you.

Let's go back to the example of reading to your child. It may be achievable, but what if you work second shift? You may not be home when your child goes to bed. The goal isn't realistic. It needs to be changed.

If you are on a medicine that causes you to gain weight, it may not be realistic to lose weight while you are on the medicine. If you want to buy a "new" used car without rust, and you live in Buffalo where there is snow and salt trucks, your goal may not be realistic.

You will need to decide what is realistic for you. Knowing your talents and skills will help you set goals that are realistic for you.

It is okay to make a smaller goal than you planned at first. You can make another goal after you achieve the first one. It is also okay to break a big goal into smaller goals. As you reach each of the smaller goals, you will be closer to your big goal.

Make Goals Timebound

A goal without a deadline is only a dream. Dreams don't often come true. Decide when you want to reach your goal. Set a date. It is a well-known fact that most people are motivated by a deadline. Even your bills have a due date to motivate you to pay them.

If you want to lose ten pounds, then set a date. Maybe you think you can lose one pound per week. Then count out ten weeks from today. That is your deadline.

Perhaps you want a new hairstyle for summer. Then set a date to have a new hairstyle by June 1. If you want a new car, when are you going to get it? Next month? Next year? In five years? You decide. Put deadlines on your goals. Without a timeframe, you probably won't reach your goals.

One more point about goals. Write them down. Put them in a place where you can see them often. A bathroom mirror works well for many people. Other people write them on a slip of paper and carry them in a purse or pocket. If you can see your goals everyday, it will remind you of what is important. Before you watch TV, glance at your goals. You might decide to study for your math test instead!

✔ CHECKPOINT 12-5

YOUR GOAL:
Get 4 or more answers correct.

Read the following goals. Make any needed changes so that they are SMART goals. An example has been completed for you. Give yourself one point for each correct answer.

- Build my self-esteem.

  Write two affirmations by the end of the week.

1. Fix my teeth.

   _____

2. Make new friends.

   _____

3. Mow the lawn.

   _____

4. Go back to school.

   _____

5. Move to a bigger apartment.

   _____

☞ *Check your work. Record your score.*

Only you can decide how you will use what you've learned in this book. No one can choose your goals for you. Choose your goals based on what is important to you. Then you will want to reach your goals because *you* set them.

There are many goals you can set to build your self-esteem and keep it high. Don't let this be the end of the book. Make it the beginning of taking action. Good luck!

WHAT YOU HAVE LEARNED

From time to time your self-esteem will slip. You can keep it high by being with positive people, accepting yourself, looking to the future, and doing things you love. You can make a difference to others if you take time to affirm them. Look for what other people do well and let them know that you noticed. To grow and develop you will need to set goals for the changes you want to make. Set SMART — specific, measurable, achievable, realistic, and timebound — goals.

ACTIVITY 12-1   **YOUR GOAL:** Get 4 points.

Write two goals for yourself to build your self-esteem in the space provided. Be sure they are SMART goals. An example has been completed for you. Give yourself two points for each goal.

- I will say two affirmations a day for the next thirty days.

Goal 1: _____

_____

Goal 2: _____

_____

☞ *Check your work. Record your score.*

ACTIVITY 12-2   **YOUR GOAL:** Get 8 or more answers correct.

Answer each of the following questions in the space provided. An example has been completed for you. Give yourself one point for each correct answer. Check your work.

- Why is it important to spend time with positive people?

  Positive people help you build and maintain high self-esteem.

1. List three ways to maintain high self-esteem.

   _____

   _____

2. What does it mean to "look to the future, not the past?"

   _____

   _____

3. Change the following statement from looking to the past to looking to the future. "I should have studied for the test. I would have done better."

   _____

   _____

4. How can you affirm another person?

   _____

   _____

5. Name two times when it is important to be specific.

   _____

   _____

6. Give one example of the words you can use to begin an affirmation to another person.

   _____

   _____

7. Give two examples of how to avoid judging others.

   _____

   _____

8. What do the letters SMART stand for?

   _____

   _____

9. Why do goals need deadlines?

   _____

   _____

10. What is one reason to write out your goals?

   _____

   _____

☞ *Check your work. Record your score.*

GLOSSARY

A

Acceptance The opposite of judgment.
Affirmation A positive statement you say to yourself that builds you up rather than tears you down.
Affirming belief A belief that makes you feel good about yourself.

C

Catastrophizing Making a mountain out of a mole hill.
Conditional love Loving someone or being loved if certain conditions are met.

D

Defensiveness Trying to protect yourself from someone else's words.

E

Evaluate To compare something to a standard.

F

Fact Reports data, is not emotional, does not judge.
Fortune telling Predicting the future. It is usually negative.

G

Global self-esteem How you feel about yourself overall.

I

Irrational belief A belief that isn't logical or true.

J

Judge A little voice inside of you that tells you all the things you are doing wrong.

Judgment Assigns value, says something is good or bad, okay or not okay.

L

Label To describe yourself, others, or situations, in a negative way.

M

Mislabel Using the wrong words to describe what you feel.

O

Overgeneralization When you take one experience and turn it into a rule about life.

P

Perfectionist A person who believes there is one right or correct way to do things.
Personal history Everything that has happened in your life up until today.
Positive focus Looking for what is positive in a situation and focusing on that.
Preference Your personal choice.

S

Self-acceptance When you can say to yourself, "I am okay."
Self-awareness The ability to act and at the same time observe yourself acting.
Self-confidence Believing in yourself.
Self-esteem How you feel about yourself.
Self-fulfilling prophecy Believing something strongly, and it comes true.
Self-image What you want other people to think of you.
Self-respect The opinion you have about yourself.
Self-talk Conversations that you have with yourself.
Self-worth Your belief that you are a valuable human being.

Skill A developed ability that requires the use of the hands, body, or mind.

Specific self-esteem How you feel about yourself in the roles you play.

T

Talent A natural ability; something that you can do easily.

U

Unconditional love is loving someone or being loved no matter what you do, say, feel, or think.

Unique One of a kind.

V

Values Your beliefs about what is right.

Value conflict Two values competing with each other.

Value judging Applying someone else's values to your life and judging yourself according to them.

Versatile You are capable of doing many things.

Visualize To see a picture of something in your mind.

INDEX

ACKNOWLEDGMENTS

For permission to reproduce the photographs on the pages indicated, acknowledgment is made to the following:

COVER PHOTO: © Robert Hale

Unit 2   p. 12: © Jim and Mary Whitmer

Unit 3   p. 24 (right): © Richard Younker

Unit 5   p. 51: © Jim and Mary Whitmer

Unit 8   p. 84: UPI/Bettmann

Unit 10   p. 109 (top): UPI/Bettmann; p. 109 (middle): UPI/Bettmann

ANSWERS

UNIT 1

CHECKPOINT 1-1, page 5
1. High
2. Low
3. Middle
4. Low
5. High
6. Middle
7. Low
8. High

CHECKPOINT 1-2, page 7
1. Values
2. Self-respect
3. Self-worth
4. Self-worth, self-respect
5. Self-esteem

CHECKPOINT 1-3, page 9
1. Esteem
2. Image
3. Esteem
4. Esteem
5. Image
6. Esteem
7. Image
8. Image
9. Esteem
10. Image

ACTIVITY 1-1, page 11
1. Low
2. Middle
3. Image
4. Self-esteem
5. Self-image
6. Self-esteem
7. Self-worth
8. Image
9. Depends
10. Values

ACTIVITY 1-2, page 11
1. a
2. b
3. a
4. b
5. a

6. c
7. b
8. c

UNIT 2

CHECKPOINT 2-1, page 15
1. F
2. F
3. T
4. T
5. F

CHECKPOINT 2-2, page 17
1. +
2. +
3. -
4. +
5. -
6. +

CHECKPOINT 2-3, page 20
1. Judgment
2. Judgment
3. Fact
4. Fact
5. Fact
6. Judgment

ACTIVITY 2-1, page 22
1. e
2. c
3. a
4. f
5. g
6. b

ACTIVITY 2-2, page 22
1. Yes
2. No
3. No
4. Yes
5. Yes
6. No
7. Yes
8. Yes
9. Yes
10. No

UNIT 3

CHECKPOINT 3-1, page 25
1. I want to quit smoking.
2. I want to read better.
3. I prefer not to make mistakes.
4. I prefer not to wait for the bus.
5. I prefer a clean house.
6. I want more friends.

CHECKPOINT 3-2, page 28
1. Steppingstone
2. Wall
3. Wall
4. Steppingstone
5. Steppingstone
6. Steppingstone

CHECKPOINT 3-3, PAGE 31
1. Macho/Tough
2. Blaming and Complaining
3. I'm the Greatest
4. Ms. Nice Gal

ACTIVITY 3-1, page 33
1. T
2. T
3. F
4. F
5. F
6. T
7. T
8. F
9. F
10. F

ACTIVITY 3-2, page 34
1. You feel the same feelings that you had when it first happened.
2. Change it to a preference or a goal.
3. You look for what you learned in the negative situation that can help you today. Difficult situations become steppingstones to the future.
4. You can decide if something that happens to you upsets you and makes you feel bad about yourself.
5. There is stress in trying to pretend you are someone, and people don't know the real you. If people like your mask self, you wonder if they would like your real self.

UNIT 4

CHECKPOINT 4-1, page 39
These are sample statements. You may have used a different word to rewrite the statement.
1. I prefer not to make mistakes.
2. I choose to be on time.
3. I want to read better.
4. I wish I had called first.
5. I choose not to loan him money.
6. I want to be more understanding.

CHECKPOINT 4-2, page 40
1. <u>None</u> of my bosses have been any good.
2. I <u>always</u> hit <u>every</u> red light.
3. <u>Nobody</u> helps me.
4. <u>Every</u> time I ride the bus, <u>all</u> the seats are taken.
5. <u>Everybody</u> in the class understands this except me.
6. Sara is <u>never</u> on time.
7. <u>All</u> the good jobs are gone.
8. <u>No one</u> works as hard as I do.

CHECKPOINT 4-3, page 43
1. fortune telling
2. labeling
3. catastrophizing
4. fortune telling
5. labeling
6. catastrophizing

ACTIVITY 4-1, page 46
1. F
2. F
3. T
4. T
5. T
6. T
7. T
8. T
9. F
10. T

ACTIVITY 4-2, page 46

I got up late this morning. <u>I should have</u> ^{should statement}
<u>gone to bed earlier</u>. <u>The bus is never on time</u>, ^{overgeneralization}

so it really didn't matter. All the way to

school, I worried about my math test. <u>"What</u> ^{catastrophizing}
<u>if I fail it? What if I flunk the course?"</u>

I'm a real <u>dummy</u> when it comes to math. ^{labeling}

I've <u>never</u> understood fractions and <u>I proba-</u> ^{overgeneralization}
<u>bly never will</u>. ^{fortune telling}

UNIT 5

CHECKPOINT 5-1, page 49

1. Belief: She believes that she can do well in school if she is prepared.
2. Consequential feeling: Frank feels overwhelmed when the car won't start.
3. Doing: Nami lifts the hood and starts working on the car.
4. Activating event: Juan's neighbor wants to borrow some tools.
5. Belief: Julie believes it is wrong to say "no" even though she wants to.
6. Consequential feeling: Rick feels comfortable saying no to his friend because he can't afford to loan the money.

CHECKPOINT 5-2, page 51

1. yes
2. no
3. yes
4. no
5. yes
6. no
7. yes
8. yes
9. yes
10. no

CHECKPOINT 5-3, page 52

1. irrational
2. irrational
3. affirming
4. irrational
5. irrational
6. affirming
7. irrational
8. affirming

CHECKPOINT 5-4, page 54

1. Expectation: It should be sunny on the weekend.
2. Expectation: Sue should remember my birthday.
3. Expectation: Tom should return my calls.
4. Expectation: The bus should run on schedule.
5. Expectation: The washer should work when I turn it on.

ACTIVITY 5-1, page 56

1. T
2. T
3. F
4. T
5. F
6. T
7. F
8. F
9. T
10. T

ACTIVITY 5-2, page 57

There are no right or wrong answers. Your beliefs are your beliefs. Look through your beliefs and ask yourself if any of them are irrational. Would you consider changing an irrational belief to an affirming one?

UNIT 6

CHECKPOINT 6-1, page 61

1. no
2. yes
3. yes
4. no
5. yes

CHECKPOINT 6-2, page 63

1. T
2. T
3. F
4. T
5. F
6. T

7. F
8. T
9. T
10. F

CHECKPOINT 6-3, page 66

These are sample answers. Your answers may be different.

1. My friend drives a 1986 car with no rust. I drive a 1980 that has a bent fender from an accident.
2. I am single.
3. Lynn can think fast in a new situation. I need time to think things through before I decide what to do.
4. When I miss my regular bus, I get to work late.
5. I read at the sixth grade level.
6. I buy my clothes at a second-hand shop and wear them for at least two seasons.
7. When someone cut in line, I didn't say anything; I allowed it to happen.
8. My neighbor lost 47 pounds on this diet. I have lost 3 pounds on the diet.

CHECKPOINT 6-4, page 68

1. yes
2. yes
3. yes
4. yes

ACTIVITY 6-1, page 69

1. Because comparing is a type of judgment. All types of judgment lower self-esteem.
2. Because sometimes when you compare yourself with someone else, you come out ahead. Then you feel better about yourself.
3. Some people look for a way that they are different from others. Then they judge the difference in their favor. The judgment makes them feel better than a whole group of people. For example, a person who has a job might judge him or herself better than anyone who does not have a job.
4. Observe differences, don't judge them.
5. You might judge the comparison you

"won" as unimportant, so it wouldn't matter if you came out ahead.

6. Don't compare people. You can evaluate a person's behavior based on a standard. You use descriptive words, not judgments, to help the person see what needs to be done differently.

ACTIVITY 6-2, page 70

Ask a fellow student or your instructor to read your paragraph. If they think you included the parts discussed in this unit, give yourself 10 points.

UNIT 7

CHECKPOINT 7-1, page 73

1. Yes
2. No
3. No
4. Yes
5. Yes
6. No

CHECKPOINT 7-2, page 75

1. P
2. P
3. R
4. R
5. P

CHECKPOINT 7-3, page 77

Some of your answers may be different from the answers that follow. Ask a fellow student or your instructor to check your answers if they don't agree with these. If they accept your answer, give yourself one point.

1. Apologize and accept your friend is hurt. Learn to think before you speak.
2. Take action, replace the flowers. Apologize.
3. Apologize and accept the consequences.
4. Take action. Wash it or get it cleaned.
5. Learn from your mistake and try again on the Bonus Checkpoint.

CHECKPOINT 7-4, page 79

1. self-awareness
2. observe

3. real self
4. like

ACTIVITY 7-1, page 81
1. T
2. F
3. F
4. T
5. F
6. T
7. T
8. T
9. T
10. F

ACTIVITY 7-2, page 82
1. Take action to fix it, apologize and accept consequences, learn from the mistake, judge yourself.
2. The ability to act and at the same time observe yourself acting.
3. Rigid, controlling, serious, stress.
4. Accept yourself for who you are; accept mistakes.
5. There is pressure to know what is perfect in every situation and then do the perfect thing. Also, human beings aren't perfect, so there is stress trying to achieve something that is impossible.

UNIT 8

CHECKPOINT 8-1, page 87
Talk over your talents with a fellow student or family member. For each talent you can list and describe, give yourself 3 points.

CHECKPOINT 8-2, page 89
Ask a friend or family member to go through your list of skills with you. Ask if he or she would add any skills you didn't list. If so, add them in the spaces provided. Give yourself 10 points for completing the Checkpoint and talking to someone about it.

CHECKPOINT 8-3, page 91
1. skills
2. powerful
3. skills
4. talent
5. talent and skills

CHECKPOINT 8-4, page 93
1. Take action. It is important for Lynn to help her mother.
2. Take no action. This can stay an undeveloped area because Keri doesn't like cards.
3. Take action. It will be hard for Jake but his son is important and the situation is serious.
4. Postpone action. Fahmi can learn the new programs after he masters what he needs for work.

ACTIVITY 8-1, page 95
Ask a family member, friend, neighbor, fellow student, or your instructor to read your 60-second commercial. If he or she agrees that you have included your skills and talents in your statement, give yourself 10 points.

ACTIVITY 8-2, page 95
1. F
2. T
3. F
4. T
5. T
6. F
7. T
8. F

UNIT 9

CHECKPOINT 9-1, page 99
1. a
2. c
3. b
4. a

CHECKPOINT 9-2, page 101
1. T
2. F
3. F
4. T
5. T

CHECKPOINT 9-3, page 103
1. I feel angry when you change plans at the last minute because I feel hurt that

I don't seem very important to you. Please call me sooner if you need to change plans so I can make other plans.
2. I feel angry about my test results because I'm afraid I won't pass the class. Can I study more and re-take the test?
3. I feel angry that you've taken a job working nights because I'm afraid we won't have any time together. I wish we would have talked this over together before you made a decision.

CHECKPOINT 9-4, page 106
1. Physically
2. Failure
3. Steps
4. Unknown
5. Psychologically
6. Admit
7. Growing

ACTIVITY 9-1, page 108
Ask your instructor or a fellow student to read your two paragraphs. Give yourself five points for each paragraph if they agree that you described the feeling word you chose.

ACTIVITY 9-2, page 108
1. F
2. T
3. F
4. T
5. T

UNIT 10

CHECKPOINT 10-1, page 112
There are no correct answers. Only you know which values are important to you. Give yourself 5 points for ranking the list of values. Give yourself another 5 points for writing down your top five values.

CHECKPOINT 10-2, page 113
There are no correct answers. Only you can evaluate your behavior for each of the values listed. Give yourself 10 points for completing the exercise.

CHECKPOINT 10-3, page 115
There are no correct answers. Only you know what value is most important to you. Ask your instructor or a fellow student to read what you wrote. They may agree or disagree with your answer. Give yourself 5 points for each answer.

CHECKPOINT 10-4, page 117
1. Because they are the values of your parents or someone else and not your values.
2. You lower your self-esteem.
3. Accepting yourself and others.
4. Try to accept your differences. Don't judge.
5. Stop value judging.

ACTIVITY 10-1, page 119
1. T
2. T
3. F
4. F
5. F
6. T
7. F
8. T
9. T
10. F

ACTIVITY 10-2, page 120
Ask your instructor, a fellow student, family member, or friend to read what you wrote. If the person who reads your essay knows you well, ask if he or she sees you the same way as you described yourself in the essay. Give yourself 20 points for writing the essay and asking another person to read it.

UNIT 11

CHECKPOINT 11-1, page 123
1. Yes
2. No
3. No
4. No
5. Yes
6. No

CHECKPOINT 11-2, page 124
1. I weigh my ideal weight.
2. I pass tests.
3. I have a new job.
4. I study for tests.
5. I read to the kids before they go to bed.

CHECKPOINT 11-3, page 126
Ask your instructor, a fellow student, friend or family member to read what you wrote. Give yourself 5 points for each paragraph that they agree describes how a Judge or Fan Club might see you.

CHECKPOINT 11-4, page 128
Ask your instructor or a fellow student to read each affirmation you wrote. Give yourself 2 points for each affirmation if he or she agrees that it is positive and written in the present tense.

ACTIVITY 11-1, page 129
1. An affirmation is positive. This means say what you want, not what you don't want. Avoid the use of the word not.
2. Affirmations use the present tense. This means don't use the future or past tense.
3. Visualize the affirmation. This means picture your affirmation in your minds eye.
4. Say your affirmation often. This means talk back to the Judge and say your affirmations every morning and night.

ACTIVITY 11-2, page 130
1. Negative
2. Future
3. Negative
4. Future
5. Future
6. Negative
7. Negative
8. Negative
9. Negative
10. Future

UNIT 12

CHECKPOINT 12-1, page 133
1. Past
2. Future
3. Future
4. Past
5. Past

CHECKPOINT 12-2, page 134
1. T
2. F
3. T
4. F
5. T

CHECKPOINT 12-3, page 136
1. I don't want to hear about Kelly.
2. I don't think those jokes are funny. Let's talk about last night's game.
3. Thank you for getting me a soft drink for my break.
4. I appreciate your friendliness and getting an answer for me so quickly.
5. Thank you for calling to tell me the doctor is running late.

CHECKPOINT 12-4, page 138
1. no
2. no
3. no
4. no
5. yes

CHECKPOINT 12-5, page 140
Your goals may be different than the ones listed. The point is to make the goal SMART.
1. Get a crown on my back molar within 60 days.
2. Make one new friend at work by the next payday.
3. Mow the lawn by Saturday night.
4. Get a college degree by the time I'm 33.
5. Move to a three-bedroom apartment by fall.

ACTIVITY 12-1, page 141

Ask your instructor or a fellow student to read your goals. If they agree that your goals are SMART, give yourself 2 points for each one.

ACTIVITY 12-2, page 141

1. Spend time with positive people; look to the future, not the past; accept yourself; do something you love.
2. You can't change the past. You can learn from the past to make changes in the future.
3. Next time I have a test scheduled, I will start studying earlier so I get a better grade.
4. Notice when he or she does something you like and tell him or her about it.
5. When you thank someone, be specific about what they did. When you set goals, be specific about your goal.
6. You can say, "Thank you," or, "I appreciate. . . . "
7. Don't put others down, don't gossip, don't laugh at sexist or racist jokes, don't take advantage of people with low self-esteem.
8. Specific, Measurable, Achievable, Realistic, Timebound
9. Without a deadline, you may not take action.
10. So you won't forget them. You can review them often.

PERSONAL PROGRESS RECORD

UNIT 1: WHAT IS SELF-ESTEEM?

Exercise	Score
Checkpoint 1-1	_____
Checkpoint 1-2	_____
Checkpoint 1-3	_____
Activity 1-1	_____
Activity 1-2	_____
TOTAL	_____

HOW ARE YOU DOING?

33 or better	Excellent
28-32	Good
23-27	Fair
22 or less	See Instructor

UNIT 3: WHERE DOES SELF-ESTEEM COME FROM?

Exercise	Score
Checkpoint 3-1	_____
Checkpoint 3-2	_____
Checkpoint 3-3	_____
Activity 3-1	_____
Activity 3-2	_____
TOTAL	_____

HOW ARE YOU DOING?

26 or better	Excellent
21 - 25	Good
16 - 20	Fair
15 or less	See Instructor

UNIT 2: THE RISE AND FALL OF SELF-ESTEEM

Exercise	Score
Checkpoint 2-1	_____
Checkpoint 2-2	_____
Checkpoint 2-3	_____
Activity 2-1	_____
Activity 1-2	_____
TOTAL	_____

HOW ARE YOU DOING?

27 or better	Excellent
22 - 26	Good
17 - 21	Fair
16 or less	See Instructor

UNIT 4: NEGATIVE THINKING

Exercise	Score
Checkpoint 4 - 1	_____
Checkpoint 4 - 2	_____
Checkpoint 4 - 3	_____
Activity 4 - 1	_____
Activity 4 - 2	_____
TOTAL	_____

HOW ARE YOU DOING?

35 or better	Excellent
30 - 34	Good
25 - 29	Fair
24 or less	See Instructor

UNIT 5: MISTAKEN BELIEFS

Exercise	Score
Checkpoint 5-1	_____
Checkpoint 5-2	_____
Checkpoint 5-3	_____
Checkpoint 5-4	_____
Activity 5-1	_____
Activity 5-2	_____
TOTAL	_____

HOW ARE YOU DOING?
40 or better	Excellent
35 - 39	Good
30 - 34	Fair
29 or less	See Instructor

UNIT 7: PERFECTIONISM

Exercise	Score
Checkpoint 7-1	_____
Checkpoint 7-2	_____
Checkpoint 7-3	_____
Checkpoint 7-4	_____
Activity 7-1	_____
Activity 7-2	_____
TOTAL	_____

HOW ARE YOU DOING?
29 or better	Excellent
24 - 28	Good
19 - 23	Fair
18 or less	See Instructor

UNIT 6: COMPARISONS AND YOUR SELF-ESTEEM

Exercise	Score
Checkpoint 6-1	_____
Checkpoint 6-2	_____
Checkpoint 6-3	_____
Checkpoint 6-4	_____
Activity 6-1	_____
Activity 6-2	_____
TOTAL	_____

HOW ARE YOU DOING?
38 or better	Excellent
33 - 37	Good
28 - 32	Fair
27 or less	See Instructor

UNIT 8: KNOW THYSELF

Exercise	Score
Checkpoint 8 - 1	_____
Checkpoint 8 - 2	_____
Checkpoint 8 - 3	_____
Checkpoint 8 - 4	_____
Activity 8 - 1	_____
Activity 8 - 2	_____
TOTAL	_____

HOW ARE YOU DOING?
42 or more	Excellent
37-41	Good
32-36	Fair
31 or less	See Instructor

UNIT 9: EXPRESS YOURSELF

Exercise	Score
Checkpoint 9 - 1	_____
Checkpoint 9 - 2	_____
Checkpoint 9 - 3	_____
Activity 9 - 1	_____
Activity 9 - 2	_____
TOTAL	_____

HOW ARE YOU DOING?
36 or more	Excellent
31 - 35	Good
26 - 30	Fair
25 or less	See Instructor

UNIT 11: POSITIVE SELF-TALK

Exercise	Score
Checkpoint 11 - 1	_____
Checkpoint 11 - 2	_____
Checkpoint 11 - 3	_____
Checkpoint 11 - 4	_____
Activity 11 - 1	_____
Activity 11 - 2	_____
TOTAL	_____

HOW ARE YOU DOING?
38 or more	Excellent
33 - 37	Good
28 - 32	Fair
27 or less	See Instructor

UNIT 10: KNOW YOUR VALUES

Exercise	Score
Checkpoint 10 - 1	_____
Checkpoint 10 - 2	_____
Checkpoint 10 - 3	_____
Checkpoint 10 - 4	_____
Activity 10 - 1	_____
Activity 10 - 2	_____
TOTAL	_____

HOW ARE YOU DOING?
67 or more	Excellent
57 - 66	Good
47 - 56	Fair
46 or less	See Instructor

UNIT 12: I LIKE MYSELF!

Exercise	Score
Checkpoint 12 - 1	_____
Checkpoint 12 - 2	_____
Checkpoint 12 - 3	_____
Checkpoint 12-4	_____
Checkpoint 12-5	_____
Activity 12 - 1	_____
Activity 12 - 2	_____
TOTAL	_____

HOW ARE YOU DOING?
32 or more	Excellent
29-31	Good
24-28	Fair
23 or less	See Instructor